Off-Topic

Off-Topic:
The Story of an Internet Revolt
(Second Edition)

G.R. Reader

Copyright © G.R. Reader, 2013
For further information, please see p. xiii.
ISBN: 978-1-304-57519-7

Digressions, objections, delight in mockery, carefree mistrust are signs of health.
— Nietzsche

To forbid us anything is to make us have a mind for it.
— Montaigne

I hope you'll appreciate that if we just start deleting ratings whenever we feel like it, that we've gone down a censorship road that doesn't take us to a good place.
— Otis Y. Chandler, Goodreads CEO

Contents

How this book got written viii
Foreword to the second edition xii
Acknowledgements xiii

I Background   1
A Review of "A Short History of Everything" 4
In the Beginning 6
A Message from Gibson's Bookstore 11

II The deletions start   13
A Review of "F*ck!" 16
By the Numbers: An Analysis of the Reviews Deleted in
    the Goodreads Policy Change 17
Why GR's New Review Rules Are Censorship 34

III Testing the limits   37
A Review of "Mein Kampf" 40
A Review of "Quotations from Chairman Mao Tsetung" 41

A Review of "The Destruction of Dresden" 42
A Review of "If I Did It" 45
A Review of "253" 48
A Review of "Logic: An Introduction" 49
A Review of "Tampa" 50
A Philosophical Discussion 54
A Review of "Editorial" by its author 56
A Review of "Martial Law" 57
A Review of "The Master and Margarita" 60
A Review of "Drive" 68
Personal, Political, Cultural: Parsing the Concept of Author Behavior in Goodreads Policy 71

IV Trying to be reasonable   79

Goodreads Get Real 82
A Review of "That's Not What I Meant!" 84

V Revolt   87

A Review of "Civil Disobedience" 90
The Hydra 94
A Hysteria of Hydras 96
A ToU-Compliant Hydra 99
An Excited YA Hydra 101
An Electronic Quotational Hydra 103
A Derridean Hydra 104
An Angry Hydra 106

G.R. McGoodreader: An Eyewitness Account 108
Wanted 111

VI The aftermath   113

A Review of "Gazelle" 116
A Review of "Moving for Dummies" 118
The Art of War: Corporate Takeover of User Rights . . . 119

VII Goodbye letters   123

The Goodreads Censorship Rap 126
My 3100 Words on the Evils Of Censorship and the Wrongness of Breaking Trust 127
Convergence Culture 138
A Retelling of Goldilocks 141
Librarian on Strike 143
A Review of "Christy" 144
A Review of "1001 Books You Must Read Before You Die" 147
One Foot Out The Door 151

VIII But what is censorship?   157

What the Founding Fathers Might Have Said to Each Other About Censorship on Goodreads 160
A Review of "Fair Play or Foul" by its author 177
A Review of "The Wonderful O" 183
Afterword 184

How this book got written

I became a member of the Goodreads online reviewing site in 2008, about a year after it started, and have since then spent a great deal of time hanging out there; more time, possibly, than was good for me. But it was so much fun. Here was a place where tens of thousands of people, from all over the world, congregated because of their common love of books. Most of the ones I chatted with were well-read, articulate, opinionated and witty. I could post a review of any book — any book whatsoever — and be sure that someone would soon add a comment to it. That usually led to an interesting online conversation, where other people would join in. Virtually the only constraint on what you could write was that you weren't allowed to post pornographic images. I wrote well over a thousand reviews, ranging in length from a few words to many pages.

In May 2013, Goodreads announced that they were being acquired by Amazon. This news was not well received. Among other things, Goodreads had stated less than a year earlier that they had broken off their relationship with Amazon, as a result of Amazon's making unreasonable demands, with the consequence that Amazon was no longer making their database available to Goodreads. This meant that many of the books listed on Goodreads now had incomplete information. Some of the people who worked as volunteer librarians on Goodreads had spent dozens or even hundreds of hours restoring the missing data, believing that this would help Goodreads stay autonomous of Amazon. They were now furious over what they saw as duplicity on the part of Goodreads management.

I did not like the news about the Amazon acquisition either, and guessed that there would soon be large changes; Amazon have always had a restrictive reviewing policy, which, at least as far as I was concerned, made it uninteresting to post reviews on their site. I had already published one collection of my Goodreads reviews as a book. I immediately put together a second collection and took all the reviews in question offline. I wasn't completely sure why I was doing this, but it somehow felt important to know that I had full control of my writing.

On September 21, 2013, a rumor started to spread that Goodreads management had deleted a number of reviews on the grounds that they contained personal attacks on the authors of the books. A clarification was soon issued by Goodreads Community Manager Kara Erickson. She said that a new policy had been put into place banning reviews which focused on "author behavior". The policy was sketchily formulated, and it was immediately apparent that it could not work. Many people began exposing its logical inconsistencies, and the US media took an interest. A brief review of *Mein Kampf*, negatively commenting on its author, was reprinted in the *Washington Post* a couple of days later. The review collected hundreds of votes, and was not deleted. Other, similar reviews were also allowed to stand.

Although only a few hundred reviews had been deleted, on a site which claimed to have over 24 million reviews posted, there was a general sense of outrage; this was, as much as anything, because of the extreme lack of clarity of the new rules. Members became increasingly creative in finding ways to test the limits. The most popular reviews were soon various forms of protest review, which in various guises questioned the good judgement of the Goodreads management, insulted them, and suggested methods for circumventing the new rules. The site has always been dominated by fads. Protesting against the rules became the new fad.

Goodreads fads tend to be short-lived, and if management had simply ignored this one it might well have run its course and disappeared. Some of the creative insults, however, appeared to have touched a raw nerve; management started deleting protest reviews, claiming in the accompanying deletion notices that the reviews were "off-topic". The site has always contained a high proportion of off-topic reviews, which are often among the most amusing ones. It was more than obvious that management was not cleaning up reviews that were off-topic *per se*; they were using this as an excuse to remove protest reviews. There was something so unutterably ridiculous about the sight of a US company deleting posts accusing it of censorship that many other people began to protest. It became common for members' avatars to feature a gag, most often a symbolic rectangle photoshopped over the mouth. Others changed their user names to include text critical of Goodreads.

In the middle of this uproar, an American author called Arthur Graham came up with a particularly clever idea: he created a fictitious book called *The Great Goodreads Censorship Debacle*, written by a fictitious author called G.R. McGoodreader. Graham's idea was a huge hit. Dozens of disaffected members posted reviews of the book, many of them insulting in the extreme towards Goodreads management. The reviews tended to collect large numbers of votes, making them very visible on the site. Management reacted two days later by deleting the book, all the accompanying reviews and comments, and McGoodreader's author page.

A tradition had already sprung up of "Hydraing": following the Greek legend of the Hydra, protesters tried to make sure that every deleted review would be replaced by at least two copies. Arthur's book was the perfect target for the most ambitious Hydra operation yet. Since I had already published two collections of Goodreads reviews, I was the obvious person to organize the work; I think four different people independently made this suggestion to me. I thought it was a wonderful idea, and asked for help. It turned out that plenty of people wanted to help. By the next day, we had a substantial group working on the project.

And then a strange thing happened. We began to collect relevant material, and the book changed before our eyes. We (or, at least, I) had originally thought of it as no more than a complicated prank. But as we read the many contributions that poured in, it became clear that this was far more than a prank. People loved the Goodreads community. They cared about the friends they had made there and the sense of being part of a world-wide family of booklovers. They were desolated by the feeling that they had been lied to and treated as merchandise by a few Silicon Valley geeks who cynically thought they could exploit those feelings to make a quick buck. They were sad and angry.

The Internet is transient. Information can be removed with a couple of mouse-clicks; it is an Orwellian dream. We have been advised, by people who claim to know about these things, that there is no point in protesting against a social network. Whoever owns the network will run it as they see fit, normally to maximize their profit margin. Members who dispute the rules will simply be thrown out. The Terms of Use are written so as not to allow them any recourse.

We have written this book to try and give a voice to the many people on Goodreads who strongly believe that the members of a social network are not a product, but a community. They have the rights one normally associates with a community, the rights that come from valuing intangible relationships between people who respect and care for each other. Nearly all of the book consists of material posted on Goodreads between September 21 2013, when the censorship policy started, and November 1, when we went to press. We have edited as little as possible, limiting ourselves to formatting, correction of obvious typos, and the occasional removal of material repeated in other posts. We want you to be able to read what members of Goodreads were writing as this little drama was going on.

We are not stupid. We understand very well that there are more important things than the question of how a social network for booknerds should be run. But the simple fact of the matter is that this is something we care about. We think other people may also care about it. If you are one of those people, we want you to know what has happened to us here, in this little corner of the Internet. Maybe you'll find that it's not completely different from what's been happening to you.

Manny Rayner
Geneva, November 1, 2013

Foreword to the second edition

In the four weeks since *Off-Topic* was released, we have seen nearly 200 reviews of it, on Goodreads and on various blogs. Over 90% of these have been positive. However, a few have been violently negative. We have in particular been accused of writing the book in order to pursue a vendetta against a few self-published authors.

We hope it will be obvious to most readers that this is absolutely not true. In order to resolve any doubts concerning the matter, we have however edited "By the Numbers", the only section in which these people were actually mentioned, so that their names no longer appear. This has in particular required the omission of one table and the anonymization of another one.

We have also corrected several typos and infelicities of formatting and presentation. In all other respects, the second edition of the book is the same as the first.

Manny Rayner
Geneva, November 29, 2013

Ceridwen Christensen
Minneapolis, November 29, 2013

Acknowledgements

This work is a collection of individual reviews, open letters and essays authored by the Goodreads reviewers known as Alfaniel, Aloha, Arthur Graham, BirdBrian, Ceridwen, Courtnie, David Lavieri, Emily May, Emma Sea, Gibson's Bookstore, Ian Gray, J. T., Kelly, Kinga, Manny, Mike Reynolds, Moonlight Reader, Nandakishore, Nathan, Notgettingenough, Paul Bryant, Richard, Samadrita, Sarah, Simon Evnine, Steph, Themis-Athena and Tracey. Each individual work is subject to a specific Creative Commons license. Please see the respective license for conditions of compliance. You are free to partially or wholly reproduce, reblog or repost any of the items contained in this work, as long as the terms of each applicable license are respected.

The individual text contributions contained in this book are attributed, copyrighted and licensed as follows:

Cover image "No more words" by Katie Tegtmeyer 2007. Design by Josephine. Shared as CC-BY 2.0 Generic.

'How this book got written' (p. viii) by Manny. Licensed under CC-BY-SA 3.0.

'Foreword to the second edition' (p. xii) by Manny and Ceridwen. Licensed under CC-BY-SA 3.0.

'A Review of "A Short History of Everything" ' (p. 4) by Manny. Licensed under CC-BY-SA 3.0.

'In the Beginning' (p. 6) by Steph. Licensed under CC-BY-SA 3.0.

'A Message from Gibson's Bookstore' (p. 11) by Gibson's Bookstore. Licensed under CC-BY-SA 3.0.

'A Review of "F*ck!" ' (p. 16) by Manny. Licensed under CC-BY-SA 3.0.

'By the Numbers: An Analysis of the Reviews Deleted in the Goodreads Policy Change' (p. 17) by Ceridwen. Licensed under CC-BY-SA 3.0.

'Why GR's New Review Rules Are Censorship' (p. 34) by Emma Sea. Licensed under CC-BY 3.0.

'A Review of "Mein Kampf" ' (p. 40) by Mike Reynolds. Licensed under CC-BY-ND 3.0.

'A Review of "Quotations from Chairman Mao Tsetung" ' (p. 41) by J. T.. Licensed under CC-BY-ND 3.0.

'A Review of "The Destruction of Dresden" ' (p. 42) by Manny. Licensed under CC-BY-SA 3.0.

'A Review of "If I Did It" ' (p. 45) by BirdBrian. Licensed under CC-BY 3.0.

'A Review of "253" ' (p. 48) by Paul Bryant. Licensed under CC-BY-ND 3.0.

'A Review of "Logic: An Introduction" ' (p. 49) by Paul Bryant. Licensed under CC-BY-ND 3.0.

'A Review of "Tampa" ' (p. 50) by Paul Bryant. Licensed under CC-BY-ND 3.0.

'A Philosophical Discussion' (p. 54) by Simon Evnine and Manny. Licensed under CC-BY-SA 3.0.

'A Review of "Editorial" by its author' (p. 56) by Arthur Graham. Licensed under CC-BY 3.0.

'A Review of "Martial Law" ' (p. 57) by Kinga. Licensed under CC-BY-SA 3.0.

'A Review of "The Master and Margarita" ' (p. 60) by David Lavieri. Licensed under CC-BY-ND 3.0.

'A Review of "Drive" ' (p. 68) by Ian Gray. Licensed under CC-BY-SA 3.0.

'Personal, Political, Cultural: Parsing the Concept of Author Behavior in Goodreads Policy' (p. 71) by Ceridwen. Licensed under

CC-BY-SA 3.0.

'Goodreads Get Real' (p. 82) by Arthur Graham. Licensed under CC-BY 3.0.

'A Review of "That's Not What I Meant!" ' (p. 84) by Manny. Licensed under CC-BY-SA 3.0.

'A Review of "Civil Disobedience" ' (p. 90) by Manny. Licensed under CC-BY-SA 3.0.

'The Hydra' (p. 94) by Manny. Licensed under CC-BY-SA 3.0.

'A Hysteria of Hydras' (p. 96) by Manny. Licensed under CC-BY-SA 3.0.

'A ToU-Compliant Hydra' (p. 99) by Sarah. Licensed under CC-BY-SA 3.0.

'An Excited YA Hydra' (p. 101) by Samadrita. Licensed under CC-BY-SA 3.0.

'An Electronic Quotational Hydra' (p. 103) by Aloha. Licensed under CC-BY-SA 3.0.

'A Derridean Hydra' (p. 104) by Nathan. Licensed under CC-BY-SA 3.0.

'An Angry Hydra' (p. 106) by Courtnie. Licensed under CC-BY-SA 3.0.

'G.R. McGoodreader: An Eyewitness Account' (p. 108) by Manny. Licensed under CC-BY-SA 3.0.

'Wanted' (p. 111) by Nandakishore. Licensed under CC-BY-ND 3.0.

'A Review of "Gazelle" ' (p. 116) by Nathan. Licensed under CC-BY-SA 3.0.

'A Review of "Moving for Dummies" ' (p. 118) by Manny. Licensed under CC-BY-SA 3.0.

'The Art of War: Corporate Takeover of User Rights' (p. 119) by Alfaniel. Licensed under CC-BY-SA 3.0.

'The Goodreads Censorship Rap' (p. 126) by Steph. Licensed under CC-BY-SA 3.0.

'My 3100 Words on the Evils Of Censorship and the Wrongness of Breaking Trust' (p. 127) by Richard. Licensed under CC-BY-ND 3.0.

'Convergence Culture' (p. 138) by Mike Reynolds. Licensed under CC-BY-SA 3.0.

'A Retelling of Goldilocks' (p. 141) by Manny. Licensed under CC-BY-SA 3.0.

'Librarian on Strike' (p. 143) by Tracey. Licensed under CC-BY-SA 3.0.

'A Review of "Christy" ' (p. 144) by Moonlight Reader. Licensed under CC-BY-SA 3.0.

'A Review of "1001 Books You Must Read Before You Die" ' (p. 147) by Emily May. Licensed under CC-BY 3.0.

'One Foot Out The Door' (p. 151) by Kelly. Licensed under CC-BY-ND 3.0.

'What the Founding Fathers Might Have Said to Each Other About Censorship on Goodreads' (p. 160) by Themis-Athena. Licensed under CC-BY-ND 3.0.

'A Review of "Fair Play or Foul" by its author' (p. 177) by Notgettingenough. Licensed under CC-BY-ND 3.0.

'A Review of "The Wonderful O" ' (p. 183) by Manny. Licensed under CC-BY-SA 3.0.

'Afterword' (p. 184) by Ceridwen. Licensed under CC-BY-SA 3.0.

With regard to any and all links to websites referenced in this book, please note that although the book's contributors have tried to include only links to such sites as they hope and expect readers to find helpful, they have no influence whatsoever on the contents of any of those websites and can, therefore, not accept any responsibility or liability for any of their contents.

In a publication such as this, it is customary for the editor and/or the publisher to point out that the various items included therein reflect merely the opinions of their respective individual authors, and their mere inclusion in the book does not constitute an endorsement of those opinions, or an acceptance of liability for them. This book constitutes an attempt to record a sample of the various and varied responses of a certain set (or subset) of Goodreads reviewers to the announcement made by Goodreads Director of Customer Care Kara Erickson on September 20, 2013, and the policies instituted by Goodreads in connection with that announcement. Just as the voices recorded here vary in tone and range from the angry to the analytical, so, too, vary the feelings of the book's contributors as to whether a documentation such as this can (or indeed should) have any potential purpose beyond its mere existence as a record. None of the contributors, however, intends this compilation, or any part of it, to cause any sort of harm. On its most basic level, it is a record of what was said (by some, not all members of the Goodreads community of reviewers). On its most ambitious, it is an attempt — perhaps a final one — to engage Goodreads in a meaningful dialogue.

Part I
Background

Before we start the story proper, we present three pieces: a short and frivolous introduction to Goodreads, followed by a couple of more factual articles that give some background. Two things in particular helped create the situation that led to Goodreads introducing censorship.

The first was the way that conflict between self-published authors and reviewers was presented in the mainstream media. Steph's piece *In the Beginning* gives a brief precis of what the story looked like from the point of view of one of the reviewers.

The second was the Amazon acquisition. Here, we reprint an open letter that was sent out by Gibson's, an independent bookstore in Concord, NH, shortly after news of the deal was made public.

A Review of "A Short History of Everything"

A Short History of Goodreads

Surveys show that nearly 40% of all Americans believe the history of literature started in 2007, when Amazon sold the first Kindle; indeed, Amazon Fundamentalists hold it as an article of faith that Jeff Bezos actually *wrote* all the world's e-books over a period of six days. This is, of course, nonsense. It has been conclusively demonstrated that literature is far older than the Kindle; books already existed thousands of years ago, which were the direct ancestors of today's e-publications. For example, careful examination reveals that *The Odyssey* and *The Gospel according to Saint Mark* are primitive versions of *Percy Jackson and the Sea of Monsters* and *Bared to You*. Similar relationships have been shown to obtain for all modern books.

Problems arise, however, from the fact that these archaic protobooks still exist today; indeed, some have adapted to the e-reader environment and begun to thrive there. It is entirely too easy for an unsuspecting reader to purchase a copy of *Pride and Prejudice*, incorrectly believing that it is part of the Twilight series. From the standpoint of formal literary theory, it is admittedly incorrect to say that *Pride and Prejudice* is "worse" than Twilight. They are simply different; neither one is "worse" than the other, since they have developed in different environments.

From a practical point of view, however, a person who buys a Jane Austen novel is almost certain to be disappointed. There are no vampires or werewolves; sex is barely even hinted at; most upsettingly of all, the book will be full of long sentences and difficult words. The combination of these factors can only lead to an intensely unpleasant reading experience, which may discourage the reader from making new Amazon purchases for days or even weeks afterwards. Particularly given the fragile state of the US economy, this is evidently not an acceptable state of affairs.

People have always exchanged recommendation and warnings with their friends, but it became clear that a more systematic approach was needed. There had to be a place where book-consumers could post advice and help each other avoid these infuriating mistakes, so that everyone could be sure of reading nothing but up-to-the-minute YA erotic paranormal romances.

Thus was born Goodreads.

In the Beginning

I remember the first time I had a review deleted on Goodreads. It was over a self-published book back in November of 2011 when Goodreads was still a relatively cool place to hang out. The book in question was by an author who displayed misogyny after advocating violence against women who wrote slash fiction. I, and many other reviewers, hastily fired off in our review spaces, some written more eloquently than my one or two sentences, which, in retrospect, was inappropriate. Needless to say, the author flagged the reviews and Goodreads responded by deleting them from the site. It was then that I was introduced to Goodreads's standard (at least, at that time) for mentioning author behavior in your review space:

> As Kara said, it's always case-by-case and the context is important. The Orson Scott Card comments would probably be allowed to remain, since they are based off of comments made in the public sphere. If they were unfounded allegations, that would be a different story.
>
> The second case is more problematic. If these members are "reviewing" the author's books just to punish her for spamming them or for some other misdeed on Goodreads (or on a blog somewhere), that's not okay. The proper way to deal with an aggressive or inappropriate author is to bring that to the attention of the Goodreads staff. We have removed reviews that said, essentially, "I will never read this book because this author was mean to my friend on Goodreads." That's a pretty clear case for removal.
>
> But again, those are general guidelines, and we deal with the cases as they come in.
> — Patrick Brown

Ah, the public sphere. How does one define that? Well, according to Goodreads it includes media outlets like magazines and newspapers. But if anyone has learned anything in the more recent author/reviewer clashes, the "public sphere" would be one of the worst places to find factual information.

2012 was the year the shit hit the fan. In January, several cases of author/reviewer clashes ensued,[1] most initiated by authors proudly waving their Be Nice[2] flags, further driving a wedge between the two groups. While Do Not Read shelves weren't new at this point in time, they certainly became more popular, much to many authors' dismay. An offhand remark in a review space could have your review deleted or hidden, but a shelf was fair game — within reason, of course. Contrary to popular belief, the Do Not Read shelves weren't created to stir more drama,[3] but instead to keep track of which books a user might want to avoid, and/or warn friends of an author with a history of attacking reviewers. After my own shelf seemed to garner more attention than I liked, I and others petitioned to Goodreads to allow private shelves for this very issue — only to be told something along the lines of "Not at this time."

So how did all of this lead up to the Goodreads we know today, the one where we have many users migrating to BookLikes and top users writing farewell posts?

1. Growing Tension From the YA Crowd

It's no secret that reviewers and authors in this area of the community has had the most negative run-ins. The reason for this is simple enough: both readers and authors are heavily involved with social media and share a very cramped space. Bumping elbows is unavoidable. Tensions were at their highest in 2012, prompting YA Highway's Veronica Roth to write a great article on the Author/Reviewer

---

[1]http://cuddlebuggery.com/blog/2012/01/05/the-first-five-days-on-goodreads/
[2]https://www.goodreads.com/author_blog_posts/973516-be-nice
[3]http://cuddlebuggery.com/blog/2012/03/15/blacklisting/

relationship[4] and YA author Hannah Moskowitz's Open Letter to Those Who Review on Goodreads.[5] Both are excellent reads if you haven't checked them out already.

2. Goodreads's Focus Shifts

For many who are confused as to why so many users are angry over the new changes to the site, it's clear to me there may be confusion on their part about how Goodreads operates. It's understandable considering this is not the same Goodreads it used to be a few years back. Even before Amazon purchased the site, things seemed to be going downhill for readers. For a site that runs off its users, for both content and catalogue maintenance, it's no shock that users, who had dedicated hours of their time for the good of the site, would be frustrated. While I myself have only a couple hundred librarian edits, there are others with *hundreds of thousands*. If you think Goodreads staff is adding books and making sure page numbers are correct, think again.

When the acquisition was announced, I thought about all the hard work librarians had put in to update thousands of books when, months previously, Amazon had disallowed Goodreads to use book data from their site. But librarians were happy to put in the extra time to update Goodreads because many were ecstatic to see Goodreads giving Amazon the one-figured salute.

As Goodreads continued to grow and author/reviewer tensions increased, they simply had to respond. Too many authors were complaining about their book pages being littered with "non-reviews", showcasing questionable author behavior to the masses. As a result, Goodreads decided to "hide" these reviews from the book page. For the record, I agreed with these changes even though I didn't particularly like where this was headed. It was a nice compromise for

---

[4]`http://www.yahighway.com/2012/01/really-long-post-about-authorreviewer.html`

[5]`https://www.goodreads.com/author\_blog\_posts/1926518-an-open-letter-to-those-who-review-on-goodreads`

readers to still have a voice and the book page to still hold reviews only. Though, admittedly, an option of a better filter system would have been ideal.

Finally, we've always known that Goodreads is a for-profit company. After all, Otis has to eat too. But what I didn't expect was to see their focus shift from helping others discover new favorite books to authors marketing their books to the biggest audience possible.

3. Poor Journalism

Does anyone do research these days? Spoiler: No. If you aren't familiar with the case of Lauren Pippa vs. Goodreads Users, I invite you to read the full story.[6] This incident sparked so much misdirected outrage, that I really believe it had a direct effect on the new policy we are under now. Many news outlets such as the Washington Post, Salon and others covered the incident based purely on Pippa's accusations without digging further, painting the Goodreads community in an unfavorable light. Though parties on both sides at times acted inappropriately, things did not happen as they were originally reported on. However, this is the "public sphere" we're talking about. If they said it happened, it must be so. #ObviousSarcasm

This, of course, further led to Nathan Bransford (a very popular and influential ex-agent) adding more flames to an already burning house in his post "The Bullies of Goodreads",[7] where he further perpetuated Pippa's story and accused harsh, critical reviews, that had nothing to do with Pippa or her book, of "dehumanizing authors." (Full disclosure: My review of *September Girls* was one of the linked reviews. Bransford later removed the links.)

Some have claimed this entire "war" has never been about negative remarks or reviews. To those people I say "bullshit." It has al-

---

[6] http://threears.wordpress.com/2013/08/29/lauren-pippahoward-throws-a-tantrum-the-internet-falls-all-over-itself-to-give-her-candy-bike-still-on-order/

[7] http://blog.nathanbransford.com/2013/09/the-bullies-of-goodreads.html

ways and will always be about the reviews. It's about some authors (mostly self-published, but not always so) believing that a negative review or harsh criticism of their "baby" will somehow crush their livelihoods by diminishing sales. It's about authors viewing critical consumers as "Big Bad Reviewers", ready to blow their book in at a moment's notice for the shits and giggles. It's about some authors still not understanding how the community works. But most importantly, it's about authors feeling they should be able to combat critical reviews written by potential customers in any way that they please. Sadly, if you are producing a good impression, this is probably not the best business model to follow.

One thing is certain, Goodreads has changed significantly, and, in my humble opinion, not for the better. With their focus primarily on helping authors sell books rather than being a place for readers, and the constant reminder that user content is only valuable as long as it doesn't conflict with their new bottom line, this place no longer feels like a "bookish home."

And this ... makes me incredibly sad.

A Message from Gibson's Bookstore

The text below was posted on the website of Gibson's Bookstore, an independent bookstore in Concord, NH. It's the kind of well-stated, well-reasoned missive that is typical of the shop.

Goodreads, a popular website that enables millions of book lovers to catalogue and discuss their favorite books with other readers, has just been bought by Amazon for an undisclosed sum. The Internet was mightily riled over this transaction. Some hailed the genius of Amazon at plucking a treasure trove of data away from competitors. Others angrily cancelled their Goodreads accounts. I was one of those, though I never really used the site. But let me briefly explain why booksellers, librarians, and traditional (legacy) publishers are put out by this transaction — why we feel insulted by those who say "well, you just didn't think of it first."

Privacy of reader information is viewed as a sacred trust by booksellers and librarians. In one historic case, Joyce Meskis, the owner of Tattered Cover in Denver, was willing to go to jail rather than reveal the reading habits of a customer who was suspected of being a drug dealer. The idea is that the First Amendment, in guaranteeing the right to free speech, also guarantees a right of privacy in acquiring and disseminating information, and protects readers from government intrusion into their reading habits.

Booksellers and librarians have similarly been in the forefront in the fight against Section 215 of the Patriot Act, which gave the government unprecedented powers to conduct warrantless searches.

No librarian or bookseller wants to give the government or anyone else access to your private information. It's in our DNA. We're a community center and a community resource. You want to be able to come in and talk to us about books. You don't want us to gossip about your reading habits to the next guy who comes in, whether that guy is your neighbor or from the FBI. We don't do it. We won't do it.

When we remember what you like, it's in service of a personal relationship. It's not "data" to "exploit." This is a profession with professional standards.

So when Amazon bought Goodreads for the purpose of data mining, so that they could target their marketing efforts at readers across the nation, we were appalled. This kind of tactic is alien to us professionally. We would never do it, and we condemn the companies that have. Both of them.

At your next book club meeting, picture me sitting quietly in the corner, taking notes on your preferences. Imagine the next day you get an email from me trying to sell you a new grill — or a book — or accessories for your Glock. That's the Amazon/Goodreads deal. It's appalling. But everywhere in the press, you'll read about the genius of Amazon.

That's not the world we want to live in. That's the world we're fighting against, every day we open our bookshops and libraries to the public. Join us.

You are not data.

Our best to you,

Michael Herrmann and the booksellers of Gibson's

Part II

The deletions start

The pieces in this section relate to the events of September 20, 2013, when Goodreads began deleting reviews. The first can be considered an executive summary suitable for busy people who want to get the global picture.

The other pieces provide further details. The second, the longest in this collection, contains Ceridwen's analysis of what actually got deleted; which reviewers, which books and which authors. Although it took some time to establish this fact, it turned out that the focus was largely on self-published authors.

The third piece, by Emma Sea, discusses the question of whether the actions of the Goodreads administrators can be interpreted as constituting censorship. From the point of view of modern literary theory, Emma argues that it is extremely reasonable to interpret them in this way.

A Review of "F*ck!"

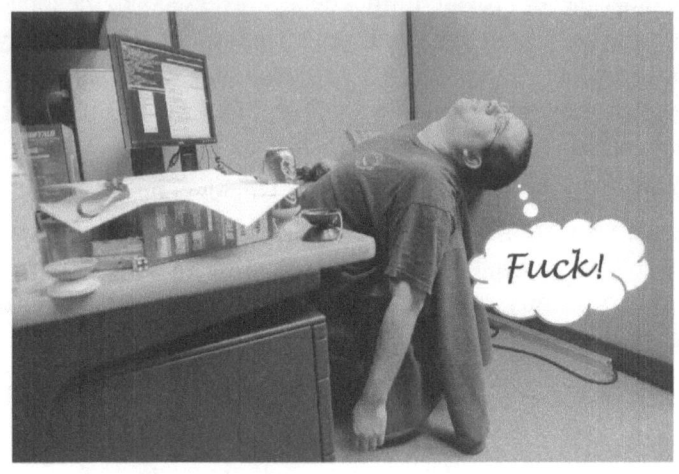

(licensed by star5112 under CC-BY-SA 2.0 Generic;
http://www.flickr.com/photos/johnjoh/368511463/)

2013: CENSORSHIP COMES TO GOODREADS

The review was posted at a point when protest reviews were being deleted on a large scale, supposedly on the grounds that they were "off-topic", and contained the following explanation:

A note to literal-minded Goodreads administrators. This review is not off-topic. *F*CK* consists of 65 cartoons, each depicting an event in world history, with an explanation of the event in question (the Big Bang, the Black Death, the Second Coming of Jesus Christ, etc) on the facing page. The only line of dialogue, repeated in each cartoon, is "Fuck!" The review is consequently a parody, intended to illustrate the nature of Rowson's rather amusing book.

Once upon a time, this kind of explanation would not have been necessary.

By the Numbers: An Analysis of the Reviews Deleted in the Goodreads Policy Change

On September 20th, Goodreads Customer Care Director Kara Erickson posted in the Goodreads Feedback group a new change in their policy. She reiterates their policy of not allowing threats or harassment and mentions some changes to the Goodreads Author dashboards. The item that gets everyone up in arms is this one:

> **[Goodreads will] Delete content focused on author behavior. We have had a policy of removing reviews that were created primarily to talk about author behavior from the community book page. Once removed, these reviews would remain on the member's profile. Starting today, we will now delete these entirely from the site. We will also delete shelves and lists of books on Goodreads that are focused on author behavior. If you have questions about why a review was removed, send an email to support@goodreads.com. (And to answer the obvious question: of course, it's appropriate to talk about an author within the context of a review as it relates to the book. If it's an autobiography, then clearly you might end up talking about their lives. And often it's relevant to understand an author's background and how it influenced the story or the setting.)

Immediately responses start flooding in, decrying this shift and asking for clarification as to what constitutes "author behavior". Kara clarifies in an edit:

> The reviews that have been deleted — and that we don't think have a place on Goodreads — are reviews like "the author is an a**hole and you shouldn't read this book because of that". In other words, they are reviews

of the author's behavior and not relevant to the book. We believe books should stand on their own merit, and it seems to us that's the best thing for readers.

Several Goodreaders note that they received emails from Goodreads with lists of book reviews and shelf names that had been summarily deleted by Goodreads. The form email used read as follows:

> Hello [Goodreader],
>
> We are contacting you to let you know your reviews of the following books have been deleted:
>
> [list of books]
>
> In the past, if a review was predominantly about author behavior and not the book, we would remove it from the community book page. Due to some recent changes to our moderation policy, reviews about author behavior will now be deleted entirely from the site.
>
> We will also delete shelves that are focused on author behavior. As such, your "due-to-author" shelf has been deleted.
>
> Please refrain from posting content like this going forward. If you continue to act in a way that is contrary to the spirit and intent of Goodreads, your account will come under review.
>
> For more information about these changes, please see the Feedback Group announcement.
>
> Best regards, The Goodreads Team

In another edit to the initial post, Kara adds:

> Thank you for all the comments so far. One concern that has come up in this thread is that the content was

deleted without those members first being told that our moderation policy had been revised.

In retrospect, we absolutely should have given users notice that our policies were changing before taking action on the items that were flagged. To the 21 members who were impacted: we'd like to sincerely apologize for jumping the gun on this. It was a mistake on our part, and it should not have happened.

When several users question what the deleted shelves "taa" and "icy-hex" even mean, and how that might have anything to do with author behavior, Kara responds:

We don't comment publicly on individual cases, but in general, what we do is look at a shelf and see how it is used in context. In any case where we have decided to remove that shelf, we are confident that the shelf was being used in a way to review author behavior.

Previously, Goodreads had just hidden reviews that focused on author behavior. A hidden review is accessible to friends, but is not listed on the main book page. Goodreads did not just delete all hidden reviews, instead they divined the intent behind the shelf names and reviews of 21 people, and then deleted their reviews. Goodreads can't publicly comment on the reviews they deleted, as I can see how that could be untoward, but the people affected can talk about the content of their reviews. These 21 people also received emails detailing the deletions, so we can know exactly what books are being flagged. I wanted to get those lists and collate the data: is there a pattern to the deletions? Are the same books and authors coming up again and again? And if I could find the 21 people who had their reviews and shelves deleted, I could ask them exactly what the content of their reviews was, and how exactly they were using their shelves.

So now I had to go about finding the 21 people who had their reviews deleted before Goodreads began sending take-down notices before deletion. 21 users isn't a lot of people, especially on a site of 20 million. (Although throwing around the 20 million users number is a little disingenuous, because the reality is that most of the activity on any given social medium is going to be concentrated into a much smaller number of people.) I already had two of the affected users in my friends list, and due to posts in the feedback thread and old-fashioned grapevining, I was able to identify six more. At this point, I put out a status update on Goodreads, which read:

> In the interests of science, I am trying to collect the lists of books deleted by Goodreads in the recent "policy change". So far, I've tracked down 8 of the 21. Can you please alert me to: 1) who got emails from Goodreads? 2) a list of their books deleted and 3) shelf names.

It didn't take me too long to realize I needed to get this update out to other social media platforms, as at least one of the people who had reviews deleted had deleted his Goodreads account, and others were staying out of Goodreads until they could download their information and then delete their accounts. I posted on Tumblr, Twitter, and Booklikes. Through a flurry of activity across several media platforms and including email, I managed to find four more users.

I was forwarded lists from these 12 people. 377 reviews were deleted in total, with the number of reviews deleted per user ranging from 1 to 129. All of their emails from Goodreads have the same wording, and the time stamps are within a short period. This would become important, as there was a second round of emails sent out to users, this time with a warning. I have excluded those lists from the data, as so far all of them have specified shelf titles only, not specific book reviews. (I have heard of one user who got a take-down notice listing specific reviews, but I have yet to hear back from her.) So, now I had lists of titles from 12 people, which seems a reasonable sample of the 21 users Kara mentions.

Unfortunately, these lists were only of book titles, and did not include the author who wrote the book. In order for this database to be meaningful in any way, I was going to have to correlate books with authors. For example, let's say that three different titles by the same author have reviews deleted off of three different users' shelves. Without knowing the author, it doesn't come out in the data that reviews of his or her book are being flagged in multiple places. Some of the titles are unique, so that eliminates guesswork. Some aren't, but I could make informed guesses by observing which were Goodreads authors who had books published in the last couple of years, or had reviews still standing that talked about the author. I assigned as many authors as I could, and then submitted the lists back to the users for correction.

In cases of a multi-author book or an anthology, I listed the author indicated by the user as the reason the book was shelved as "do-not-read". In cases where a writer works under several pen names, I listed their real name. (Or maybe more clearly, I listed the name that the writer uses publicly, even if it is a pseudonym too. My aim was to have all books written by the same person show up together, not determine what name is on the driver's licence. That's never important information.)

So this is my first large disclaimer: **The list of titles comes directly from the Goodreads emails, but the list of authors assigned to those books is constructed data**. In some cases, the user simply couldn't recall which of the dozens of books entitled *Inhale* or *Truth* she had decided not to read. And the first disclaimer brings me to my second disclaimer: **this list of authors should not be taken as a hit list**. Despite Goodreads's surety that they were only deleting reviews based on author behavior, this was not the case for many of the titles listed. Before I get into specifics, though, I should probably talk about what these reviews looked like.

There are a lot of things we can't know for a fact, because obviously the reviews are gone, but I asked all the users if the reviews in question had ratings, or if the review field had any content. Almost all of the reviews in question had no ratings. All of these users adhere to a personal policy of not rating books they haven't read, with the exception being books that they have read parts of. The only books that had ratings had been at least partially read. Here I would like to note that Goodreads does not have a policy against rating books that you have not read, as that would be both unenforceable and impossible to prove.

I have seen users bemoan that these reviews are somehow skewing the ratings for books, but I would like to point out two things. First, we are dealing with a few hundred reviews against the tens (and possibly hundreds) of millions of reviews on Goodreads. There is no way their removal is going to have a statistical effect. Second, there are thousands of users doing things like "rating on excitement" for unreleased books. Take something like *Black Ice*, Becca Fitzpatrick's book which has a publication date more than a year from now. As far as I'm aware, there are no advanced reader copies, and likely the only people who have read this are Fitzpatrick's friends and family, if even a completed manuscript exists. *Black Ice* has an average rating of 4.23, which is completely unheard of. 67 users have given it a 5-star rating, versus four who have given it a one. If you want to talk about skewed ratings — and I would like to note right now that ALL ratings are subjective by their very nature and therefore meaningless as some kind of objective metric — then you should start with the overwhelmingly positive ones.

For example, a comment from Goodreads CEO, Otis Chandler, in a Goodreads Feedback thread about pre-ratings:[8]

> Interesting thread! I agree that it's a shame some books have to suffer ratings that clearly are invalid. However I can't think of a way to prevent it, and I didn't see any ideas in the thread either (I did skim though). I hope

---

[8]http://www.goodreads.com/topic/show/300795-disabling-ratings-reviews-before-a-book-s-publish-date?page=2\#comment_14538563

you'll appreciate that if we just start deleting ratings whenever we feel like it, that we've gone down a censorship road that doesn't take us to a good place.

As for manuscripts or yet-to-be-published books, I have no problem with them being in the database. It's kind of cool to have a record of in-progress books, and I don't think it hurts anything. I do think we'd need to remove any that weren't serious in their intent to be a finished book one day.

When there was content, the review content was generally terse, from quick dismissals to "not for me" to "see comments" to a link or screencap to whatever the controversy was surrounding the book. Many of these controversies, indeed, had to do with the broadly defined issue of author behavior. These controversies range from books being pulled from publication for plagiarism, racist or homophobic statements made by the author, the author's conviction on the charges of owning child pornography, downvoting campaigns instigated by authors or agents, the doxing of reviewers by authors, down to just a bunch of dumb stuff authors occasionally say out loud. I have already written at length about how these "author behaviors" are not equal, but just to reiterate: noting a book has been pulled for plagiarism, for example, is about the book's unoriginal content, not about the author's behavior as a word thief. Noting a children's book author is convicted of child pornography is the kind of author behavior that has a direct import on the content. Many, many people are currently boycotting Orson Scott Card for his political views, and deciding not to read the books by authors because of their beliefs is a political act Goodreads has no business getting in the middle of. The rest I'm going to shelve for the moment, and get onto the next point.

Additionally, some of the books were shelved "do-not-read" not because of the actions of the author, but because the book looked bad to the user. These are a vanishingly small number though. The other large minority of reviews deleted were shelved because the book was pulled-to-publish fan fiction, e.g. *Fifty Shades of Grey*. A pulled-to-publish fan fiction is one where a freely available fan fiction is pulled, the content lightly edited — often a search-and-replace with the names "Bella" and "Edward" substituted for other names, not to be too snarky here — and then the book put up for sale. P2p books, as these are referred to, are a controversial topic, but I can't really call the path to publication and the source of the plot lines "author behavior", except in a way that nullifies most of literary criticism. (Also of note: no reviews of Fifty Shades were deleted, though I'm sure I could find you many that note its p2p status and not much else.) Whether you regard p2p novels as ethical or not, the information that a book is p2p is not about the author at all.

As far as the content of the review, most indicated that they had nothing in the review field for most of their reviews. Often the comments about the author behavior were occurring solely in the comment threads, as there was literally nothing — not a rating, nothing in the review field — about author behavior at all. From personal correspondence with reviewer rameau:

> I kept the specifics in the comment field from the moment GR first announced they weren't allowing any non-book related information about authorial behaviour in reviews.

Or from Miranda, whose reviews constitute 129 of the reviews deleted, a sizable minority:

> None of those books had an actual text review or a rating. Only shelved by me, but all had screenshots or links in the comments.

If there was no content — no rating, no statement to the effect of "The author is such a dick. I'm not even going to read it!" — then what Goodreads has done here is delete forums on which Goodreaders have discussed their personal boycotts of selected authors, discussions which are going on all over the site right at this moment, and have likely increased exponentially since the vaguely worded new policy about author behavior. **Though Goodreads is claiming this is about review content — such as the hypothetical review example from Kara "this book is by an a**hole and you shouldn't read the book because of that"** — many of these reviews literally had no content, and Goodreads has taken action **against review** *threads*. I am appalled by this, and you should be too. More than anything else about this debacle, this is the thing I would like you to come away with: **Goodreads has deemed the comment threads of a user's review space actionable to the point of deleting the entire comment thread.**

The Database

But let's move away from the self-reported data into the actual data. A searchable database can be found online,[9] and there are screencaps I'll get up at some point to ensure that if there's some kind of vandalizing of the data, a record of it in its original form is extant. (I don't even mean to sound paranoid, but after the copious googling it took to compile these authors — not all, not even most, but a virulent few — I am actually feeling worried that someone might try to vandalize the data.)

So, some very basic numbers:

Number of delete lists	12
How many reviews deleted, in total	377
Average number of books deleted, per user	31.4

The number of reviews deleted, by user:

Archer	6	Bitchie	3	Carla	76	Jane	9
JennyJen	72	Kara	17	Linda	1	Mirage	10
Miranda	129	rameau	5	Ridley	36	Steph	13

---

[9] https://skydrive.live.com/view.aspx?Bsrc= Share&Bpub=SDX.SkyDrive&resid=36CE06E5F5107064\ %21116&cid=36ce06e5f5107064&app=Excel&authkey=\% 21AtBYDdneqNLgi_M

As you can see, the number of reviews deleted by user varies wildly. Three users, Carla, JennyJen, and Miranda, had 277 reviews deleted between them, which constitutes almost three quarters of the number of deleted reviews. This looks incredibly personal.

Here is a graphic of the number of reviews deleted by user:

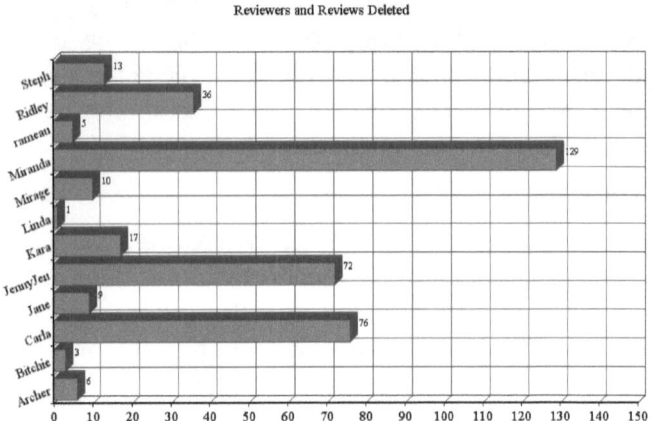

(And a quick note on user names: several of these users asked that I keep their Goodreads screen name out of this. I have assigned pseudonyms to three of them, and shortened one screen name in the interests of brevity.)

A Statistical Sampling of Authors

Overall, the 377 reviews on this list were written by 174 authors, giving us an average of about two books for each author deleted. The actual deleted number range from 1 to 14. It's fairly easy to sort through the lists and find the author who has the most books deleted, but this isn't statistically important information. Usually that is an indicator that the author has written a lot of books, and/or the author was shelved heavily by one user only. The more important data is this: **what authors' books are showing up on multiple delete lists.** Again, I want to reiterate: **this list of authors is not a hit list. It is simply the authors whose books turned up on multiple**

delete lists, for whatever reason. In doing my research, I had to unearth the controversies that surrounded each of these writers, and I felt some of the situations were silly or overblown, while plenty of them had merit. In other words, I used my own judgement about the information. To quote rameau again:

> BBA [badly behaving author] note doesn't stop me from reading a book (see Jamie McGuire and Orson Scott Card), it's supposed to stop me from spending money without serious consideration.

The list below notes the name first, and then the number of users' delete lists their books were on. Since some of these people have objected to being mentioned here, and their actual identities are not important to the argument, we have anonymized all the names.

Author-1	5	Author-2	5
Author-3	4	Author-4	4
Author-5	4	Author-6	4
Author-7	4	Author-8	3
Author-9	3	Author-10	3
Author-11	3	Author-12	3
Author-13	3	Author-14	3
Author-15	3	Author-16	3
Author-17	2	Author-18	2
Author-19	2	Author-20	2
Author-21	2	Author-22	2
Author-23	2	Author-24	2
Author-25	2	Author-26	2
Author-27	2	Author-28	2
Author-29	2	Author-30	2
Author-31	2	Author-32	2
Author-33	2	Author-34	2
Author-35	2	Author-36	2
Author-37	2		

The reason why these 37 authors out of the 174 total are interesting is that they showed up on multiple delete lists. Rather than go through all of the authors and try to find the controversy behind their do-not-read status, I have used this group as a statistically important sampling. **Of the 377 reviews deleted, 240 were for reviews of books by these 37 authors. 64% of the reviews deleted are covered by this list of 37 authors**. All of the graphs going forward deal with these authors only. If anyone wants to do a more complete sample, the database is freely available.

The following graphic, "Who published these books?", shows how many authors on multiple delete lists were indie, with small presses, or with Big Six publishing houses. Sometimes the exact affiliations are hard to parse, and decisions had to be made about whether Big Six distribution was the same as Big Six publishing, etc. You are welcome to parse this chart yourself. Either way, the chart shows the general trends. We're dealing with largely self-published books here.

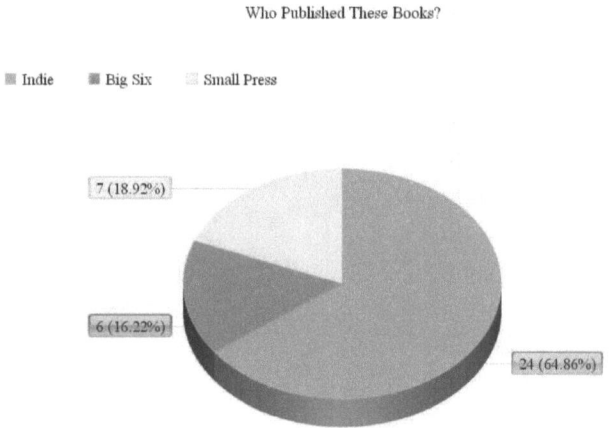

Who Published These Books?

■ Indie ■ Big Six ▫ Small Press

7 (18.92%)
6 (16.22%)
24 (64.86%)

Although the reviewer/authors conflicts have been sometimes been characterized as occurring in the Young Adult readership more than others, when you look up the genre of the books affected (the graphic

"Deleted books by genre"), that doesn't turn out to be true. It is a large minority, but plenty of other genres are represented. This is not a boutique issue. Some books are in multiple categories or genres, which is why these categories add up to more that 37.

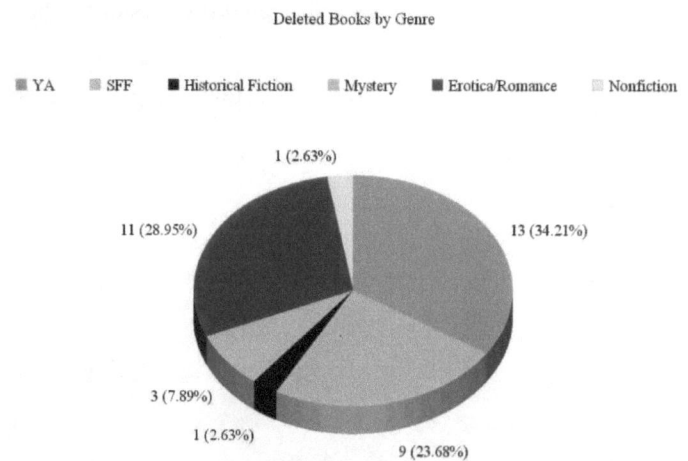

Deleted Books by Genre

Next up (the graphic "Why were they shelved?" on the following page) we have the nature of the controversy that landed the author in question on multiple users' do-not-read lists. Admittedly, this involves some guesswork, but generally the controversies were easily googleable, and I relied on the reportage of the people involved. I've broken the kind of controversy into categories, based on my own sense of how they are different. The categories are:

- Political: racist, sexist and homophobic statements made by author, in addition to one instance of the author being convicted of owning child porn.
- Marketing: use of sockpuppets for rating inflation, spamming bloggers, spamming in general.
- Reviewer conflicts: personal attacks against readers/reviewers,

downvoting campaigns instigated by either authors or proxies, impolitic statements.

- p2p fiction or plagiarism: either the author has written pulled-to-publish fan fiction, or there are allegations of plagiarism either in the book, or in sockpuppeted reviews of the book.

(Several authors showed up in multiple categories, just as a clarification.)

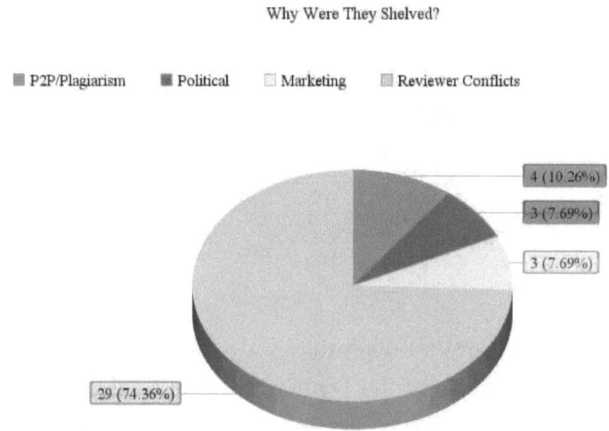

The elephant in the room here is affiliation with the website Stop the Goodreads Bullies. I urge you strongly not to give Stop the Goodreads Bullies traffic. Their initial postings were all doxings of reviewers. (Doxing is a term referring to dropping documents, or outing all of the personal information of an Internet user, from spouses to children, to where people lunch.) There are a lot of arguments on the legitimacy of doxing, but I think most reasonable people would agree that the response to a negative — not even libelous — review should not be the open posting of a reviewer's address. That's not the counter of speech by more speech, but with an implicit threat. It's not that you're wrong, and here's why; it's that I know where you live. STGRB's tactics in using out of context screenshots can be found on my own thread,[10] and you can read the entire context yourself.[11] I apologize in advance for how much cussing I do, in general.

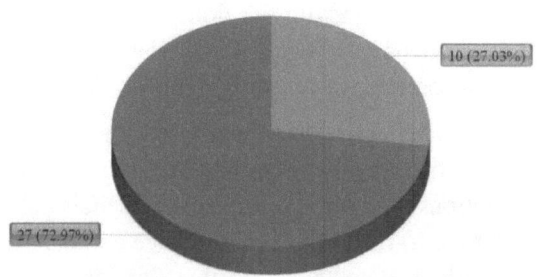

STGRB Affiliated?

A sizable minority of the reviews deleted were authored by STGRB affiliated authors, and in some cases I'm struggling to understand why Goodreads is going after reviews of books by authors they have actually banned from their site. By the numbers, these are largely self-published authors. I don't even mean to sound snarky, but who even cares about these writers in the larger literary context? Maybe it's ridiculous to give these writers platform by shelving their books do-not-read and linking to their myriad social media meltdowns, but it is so much more ridiculous to delete the discussion of these events. Goodreads is a social media platform, and this seemingly personal, yet also arbitrary, deletion of conversations should give the average Goodreader pause.

---

[10] http://s181.photobucket.com/user/shellnick2003/media/ScreenShot2013-10-02at90952PM_zpsaa083080.png.html

[11] http://www.goodreads.com/user_status/show/33394858

Whether you think these conflicts have any merit, whether you think doxing is legitimate, whether you think sockpuppets are a valid marketing strategy, it makes no sense to me that users cannot be allowed to exchange this information about the professional, personal, political, criminal, and sometimes, just sometimes, the literary merit of living authors. It is not just a marketplace of ideas, but an actual marketplace, and often the only power we have as consumers, as citizens, is in where we spend our hard earned dollars. Where we spend our hard earned dollars on a leisure activity. The only vote we have sometimes is the one with our dollars, and Goodreads coming in and stifling discussion of who users believe merit their time and cash is, and I'm sorry for the cussing, bullshit.

While I was writing this post, Goodreads "announced" on their Feedback thread that they were going to try to reinstate the reviews lost in the deletions, and some clarification of their policy. Frankly, I haven't had time to read this, and I'll leave its consideration for a later date. The reviewers who were subject to deletion also received the following email:

> Hi [Goodreader],
>
> We are contacting you to let you know we are working on retrieving the content that was deleted from your account on September 20. We're very sorry about how that was handled. In retrospect, we should have notified you and provided you with a copy of your content when we deleted the reviews/shelves.
>
> We also mistakenly deleted your shelf called "due-to-author". We know we were not clear in our previous response about this. A "due-to-author" shelf fits within our guidelines and is allowed on the site. We've discussed this in more detail with our engineers, and while the reviews have been completely deleted from the database, it turns out we can retrieve the content through back-up servers. We will email it to you for

your personal records as soon as the import completes in a week or two. Feel free to re-import your "due-to-author" shelf, but please note that the content that violated our guidelines cannot be re-posted on Goodreads.

Sincerely, The Goodreads Team

So, sorry we deleted your reviews, but they are still illegal according to a policy we absolutely refuse to clarify. If you look at the data, reviews are being arbitrarily and personally deleted, according to no standard I could discern. I leave it to you, fellow Goodreaders, to make sense of these numbers.

A quick note of thanks

I have been using the word "I" though this essay, but that is inaccurate. This database would not have come to be without the help of dozens of people. Thanks to:

The 12 people who forwarded me their delete lists, anyone who passed notes, sent me links, and otherwise made this social media social; for technical help, a shout out to DMS who built the spreadsheet, and sj for making graphs, and Ziv for number crunching; general thanks to Steph and Wendy Darling for link-farming and karen for reader's advisory, plus just dozens and dozens of people who found me and told their stories. As sickened as I am by this action by Goodreads, I am cheered by the overwhelming power of concerned people acting together. Single tear, guys.

Why GR's New Review Rules Are Censorship

Late on Friday September 20 (US time) Goodreads announced a change in review and shelving policy, and immediately started deleting readers' reviews and shelves. In doing this, they became censors. Limiting readers' ability to discuss the cultural context of a book is censorship designed to promote authors' interests.

Prior to this, Goodreads had always maintained that shelves were up to a reader, and that, short of abuse (which could be flagged) so were reviews. Now Goodreads states that reviews and shelves must be about the book, and unrelated to the author, unless it is "relevant," such as a biography.

Goodreads denies this is censorship, but rather "setting an appropriate tone for a community site."

Goodreads states, "we haven't deleted any book reviews in regard to this issue. The key word here is "book". The reviews that have been deleted — and that we don't think have a place on Goodreads — are reviews like "the author is an a**hole and you shouldn't read this book because of that". In other words, they are reviews of the author's behavior and not relevant to the book."

In literary critism there are several different ways of approaching a book. In one corner there's practical criticism, New Criticism, formalists and structuralists. These types of approaches look only at the form and, well, structure of a book. In these kinds of reviews "it is the reader who ... is in the end, in the absence of authorial control, left alone with the text,"[12] and the reader limits themself to "the words on the page."[13]

This would appear to be Goodreads' approach to reviewing, when they say, "We believe books should stand on their own merit."

---

[12] Bertens, H. (2008). Literary theory: The basics (2nd ed.). London, UK: Routledge, p. 59.
[13] *Idem*, p. 61.

From the 1970s on a new approach, or rather, new approaches, to literary criticism arose, which examine the social, political, economic, and historical contexts to any particular book.

Feminist literary criticism discusses books in terms of the gendered roles and positions of the author, character, setting, or arena of cultural production.

Marxist criticism sees a text as a tool in struggle for economic and social capital. We might buy a book, for which we have to turn ourselves into a unit of production, or we might be given an online fic for free, and in return we give the author social capital, and reviews might discuss aspects of this process.

In postcolonial criticism you might examine the author's position as a product of a hybrid culture: a mix of indigenous and colonizing forces.

What all postmodern approaches to reviewing books have in common is that they acknowledge that a book does not exist in a vacuum: it did not spring, fully-formed, into being. An author wrote it as a particular form of cultural and economic production in a particular society at a particular time.

Goodreads states, "Some people are perhaps interpreting this as you can't discuss the author at all. This couldn't be further from the case. The author is a part of the book and can certainly be discussed in relation to the book. But it has to be in a way that's relevant to the book. Again, let's judge books based on what's inside them."

A member's review of an Orson Scott Card book was deleted following the Goodreads announcement, because it focused on Card's well-known anti-gay and anti-gay marriage views. This fits within a wider cultural call to boycott the upcoming film.

In a queer Marxist critique of this book we would absolutely want to state that the funds you use to purchase it are in part used by the author to fund anti-gay marriage organizations and activities. Of course Card is allowed to do this: he is free to believe what he wishes. But equally an informed reader may not wish to financially support him in these acts. Card's anti-gay platform is not directly relevant to the "words on the page" that Goodreads wants reviews to be about, but it is directly related to the social and cultural context of the book.

By deciding what is, and is not, allowed to be discussed in a review, by removing discussion of social context, and saying that only the words on the page count, Goodreads is ignoring fifty years of development of literary criticism, and is engaging in censorship.

This leaves us in a space where indeed, as an astute reader has already pointed out, a review of *Mein Kampf* that called Adolf Hitler an anti-Semitic asshole would break Goodreads's new review guidelines and Terms of Use.

Yes, Adolf Hitler is a straw man, but what has equally been banned by Goodreads are shelves that indicate an author has "behaved badly." This might be an author who emails the reviewer offering free books if their neutral review is edited to be more favorable, or an author whose fans flame a negative review. One of these may be out of the direct control of the author, but both are about the social context of the book.

Books are one part of a vast multi-media network of tweets, blogs, films, magazines, statuses, television shows, face-to-face conversations, Skype chats, and emails. Pretending that the words on the page are unconnected to any of the rest of modern communication is ... well, I want to say it's absurd, but it is not absurd. It is marketing.

Goodreads's new rules are a fundamental shift that moves the site from a place for genuinely open discussion and engagement, to one that places the requirements of authors above the requirements of readers.

It is censorship.

Part III

Testing the limits

The ban on negative discussions of author behavior in reviews was not well received. Surprised and annoyed, many reviewers decided to stress-test the new policy in various imaginative ways.

Mike and J.T. were quick to post negative reviews of books by Adolf Hitler and Mao Tsetung; Mike's was allowed to stand, while J.T.'s was deleted. Manny wrote a review of a book by the Holocaust denier David Irving. BirdBrian reviewed O.J. Simpson's quasi-confession *If I Did It*, and Ceridwen a book by plagiarist Jonah Lehman. All of these were left undisturbed.

Paul Bryant used a different approach. He first posted a review of the experimental novel *253*, in which he insulted the book while heaping fake compliments on the author. This was allowed. His next review, however, pretended to discuss a book on logic while in fact pointing out the lack of logic in the new rules; it was deleted on the claimed grounds of being "off-topic". In a third round, he posted another intentionally off-topic review, in which he compared ten books based only on their first lines. This time, his effort was allowed to stand.

Simon Evnine, a professor of philosophy in real life, also took a logical route. He reasoned that it should be just as wrong to post exaggerated and untrue positive statements in a review as exaggerated and untrue negative ones. His test review provoked a bizarre exchange with the author, but was accepted.

Arthur Graham, an author of William Burroughs style fiction, stayed in character by launching a furious *ad hominem* attack on himself. Kinga, who grew up in Communist-era Poland, wrote a delicate satire elliptically comparing Goodreads policy with Stalinist censorship; David Lavieri's clever pastiche of Bulgakov's *The Master and Margarita* was similar in inspiration, though stylistically very different. Ian Gray pretended to review *Drive* while actually parodying a Goodreads job ad. All these reviews were allowed to stand.

In the final piece, Ceridwen summarizes the absurdity of the situation that Goodreads management had now constructed for itself.

A Review of "Mein Kampf"

This author is such a dick. I'm not even going to read it!

The review was quoted in the September 23, 2013 edition of the Washington Post, with the word "dick" replaced by "[jerk]"

A Review of "Quotations from Chairman Mao Tsetung"

So apparently Goodreads want to remove, without warning, any review that doesn't actually talk about the book (well more or less) but attacks the author. Not hide, not ask the author nicely to change, just a total removal. So I'm not actually going to write a review about this book, I'm testing the waters (inspired by certain friends) to ask whether we can all show Goodreads just a little how ridiculous and unprofessional the sudden changes to its terms of service are by posting reviews and shelves like this. I mean, really, what kind of grey area are we going into? Are some of the excellent humorous reviews out there just going to disappear, hence removing some of the fun of this site?

If this review still stands by the same time next week as it is (including shelves): well, I'll take it that Goodreads are making empty statements and that is that — more for the sake of legalities.

Also, Chairman Mao was a rather vile dictator who killed off millions of his people. More of his own people than Hitler committed genocide. I can't see his ego getting stroked from beyond the grave...

Which is why I want to further add: why is Goodreads making this effort to stroke author egos? I see more directed at readers here. Yes, maybe some shelves are pointlessly rude. But not giving people a chance to save content and change (doing a backflip) is just unethical. And Mao is still evil.

UPDATE: Still nothing from Goodreads on what they've done so unprofessionally. An amendment and apology couldn't be that hard, right?

The review was deleted by Goodreads on the grounds that it was "potentially off-topic".

A Review of "The Destruction of Dresden"

Why I Refuse to Read David Irving

Over the last few days, there have been extensive protests concerning the new Goodreads policy, which is widely interpreted to mean that people who post reviews criticizing authors are liable to have them deleted. The most visible of these protests is Mike's review of *Mein Kampf*, where Mike calls Adolf Hitler a dick and says he refuses to read his book. The review has already attracted more than 300 votes and 150 comments.

We all know that Hitler was a monster and that *Mein Kampf* is one of the most hateful and dangerous books ever written. Mike's warning is funny because it is so obviously superfluous. But there are other cases where the truth is not quite as generally known, and this is one of them. David Irving was famously found guilty of being a Holocaust denier in a high-profile trial which bankrupted him. He was later sentenced to three years in prison by an Austrian court on charges of "trivialising, grossly playing down and denying the Holocaust". If you look at the Wikipedia article on Irving, you will find the following quote from Christopher Browning, a historian who is an expert on the Holocaust:

> Not one of [Irving's] books, speeches or articles, not one paragraph, not one sentence in any of them, can be taken on trust as an accurate representation of its historical subject. All of them are completely worthless as history, because Irving cannot be trusted anywhere, in any of them, to give a reliable account of what he is talking or writing about. ... if we mean by historian someone who is concerned to discover the truth about the past, and to give as accurate a representation of it as possible, then Irving is not a historian.

The same article contains interesting material about this book, *The Destruction of Dresden*, which was written before Irving's views on the Holocaust became widely known and became a bestseller. Again, I quote:

> In the first edition, Irving's estimates for deaths in Dresden were between 100,000 and 250,000 — notably higher than most previously published figures. These figures became authoritative and widely accepted in many standard reference works. In later editions of the book over the next three decades, he gradually adjusted the figure downwards to 50,000–100,000. According to the evidence introduced by Richard J. Evans at the libel trial of Deborah Lipstadt in 2000, Irving based his estimates of the dead of Dresden on the word of one individual who provided no supporting documentation, used forged documents, and described one witness who was a urologist as Dresden's Deputy Chief Medical Officer. The doctor has since complained about being misidentified by Irving, and further, was only reporting rumours about the death toll. Today, casualties at Dresden are estimated as 22,700–25,000 dead.

Yet looking at the five reviews here on Goodreads, I see that four of them uncritically accept Irving's account and praise the book.

If I were willing to spend several months or years of my life on the task, I could do my own digging around and try to come to an independent conclusion. I am unlikely to do this; it seems to me, just on the basis of the few articles I have read, that the facts are pretty clear. Irving has been repeatedly unmasked as a Nazi sympathizer and a serial liar. He has tried to defend himself against these charges in court, and he has failed miserably. Yet, somehow, people are not as aware of his true nature as they should be.

I do not see anything unethical about posting this negative review of Irving, and it may conceivably have some value in making unsuspecting people more critical of his book. I am concerned about Goodreads policies which may lead to reviews of this kind being deleted without warning. They strike me as utterly wrong, and moreover as yet another example of how modern technology distances us from the consequences of our actions. If people wrote their reviews on paper and put them into a real, physical library, I am sure that the Goodreads administrators would be very reluctant to pull them down from shelves and burn them. When you can get rid of a piece of writing just by clicking on a few links, there's a temptation to believe that it's less serious. But it isn't. It's just less clear what you've done.

I am absolutely against book-burning in all its forms. I do not want David Irving's books burned, or even *Mein Kampf*. But I do want people to know that the authors of these books are racist liars, and I, at least, refuse to read them.

A Review of "If I Did It"

Censorship sucks, AND it often doesn't even work

Let's get this part out of the way first: I thought the book was poorly written. I thought the grammar was at times awkward, and some of the things said were illogical. I found spelling errors on pages 4, 92, and 9024.

"If I Did It". Kinda clever what he did there, isn't it? The whole premise of the book is a hypothetical, so it isn't really an admission of wrongdoing — even though it describes step by step exactly how O.J. would have committed the crime he was accused of ... you know, "if" he did it.

Like most people in America, I followed this trial with interest, and I feel confident based on what I learned that O.J. Simpson is guilty of Nicole Simpson and Ron Goldman's murders.

My understanding is that O.J. wrote this book to get money to help pay his legal bills from the trial, although most of the money now goes to the Goldman family, because they won a civil case against him. So as I see it, this book was written to help a murderer — who eluded justice — to further profit from his crime ("further" beyond whatever murderous bloodlust of the moment it satisfied.)

That makes me really despise this author's behavior.

But of course we all know that I can't just come out and trash the book based on how I feel about the author's behavior. That would violate Goodreads's Terms of Use.

Of course **If** I didn't read the book, and I posted a 1 star review of it anyhow, I'm not entirely sure how Goodreads would know this. And **If** I wanted to write an excoriating review that appeared to be "about the book", I could skim the brief description on the book's page for a few central points and themes, couldn't I? I could find a few names to drop, and probably cobble together a review that sounded like I had read the book. (**If** I didn't read the book, but of course I totally did.)

Naturally, I'd have to keep the review "about the book". I'd have to say the writing was bad, things didn't make sense, it was boring, etc, etc. But it would be easy enough to do, **If** I felt strongly enough about it.

So what's my point?

My point is that back in the Goodreads "Before Censorship Era" (BCE), I could have written a nasty review about the author, and put it on a shelf called "authors who profit from murder". I could have openly admitted that I never read the book, and readers could take that into consideration when they read my review. Goodreaders would see my honest opinions for what they are, and they could make their own mind up about whether my thoughts on the author are justified, and whether they agree, and whether they should avoid the book. Reviews from the BCE were more likely to be open and honest, even if they were exceedingly negative.

Now we are in the Censorship Era (CE). **If** I feel strongly about a book based on its author, there's no way of stopping me from writing a terrible review about it; I just have to keep some rules in mind, to escape detection. With 20 million users on the site, it seems unlikely that GR could realistically track down and identify all the reviews which appear to be about the book, but which are really driven by other motives. Not going to happen. It is an ironclad certainty that reviews like that WILL be posted in the future, and they WILL escape official detection.

The thing is, with all of the honesty of the BCE lost, how is anybody to know which reviews are reliable, and which ones are effectively wolves in sheep's clothing? Goodreads' new policies (or old policies with new implementation practices) doesn't eradicate "because-of-the-author" reviews; it merely drives them underground. And in doing so, it makes ALL reviews suspect.

The Goodreads of BCE had some nasty author-reader blowups, but for the most part the reviews everybody had such bad feelings about were easy to identify, and they didn't call the integrity of other reviews into question. In the Goodreads of the CE, EVERY review is suspect. You can't tell which is honest and which is an imposter.

It cheapens the value of reviews and thus of the site. While Goodreads/Amazon doesn't care about the free expression of ideas, or building a community of readers, you can bet they care about the value of the site, because that affects revenue.

So what has Goodreads achieved by censoring reviewers? It appears they have reduced the value of their own product (i.e. their precious "author packages"), and they have not prevented even a single reviewer from posting negative, because-of-the-author reviews, including of books the reviewer hasn't read.

To go back to where we came in: not only does censorship suck, but it often doesn't even work.

A Review of "253"

This was tedious postmodern whatever who cares "experimental" crap of the worst sort.

Although I would like to make it clear that I think the author was, is, and always will be a really nice person.

This book was so grindingly obvious in all its techniques and the "shock ending" was telegraphed so far in advance a person in a deep coma would have sussed it by page three if their loved one had started reading it to them. Actually, it would have cured the person in the deep coma, because they would have woken up and yelled "please stop reading, please, I'll do anything, just stop".

But as I say, the author is a really really sweet natured person who as I understand is very kind to little children and dogs, but not in a creepy way, in a good way.

I really hated this thing.

But the author is one of my favourite human beings. And yours too.

This review was only about the book.

A Review of "Logic: An Introduction"

Another hapless Goodreads employee contemplates his in-tray.

It contains reviews which have been flagged for focussing on author behaviour, which is not allowed ("we will now delete these entirely from the site").

Our poor Goodreads employee now has to read through all these flagged reviews to figure out if they do indeed contravene the policy. It's a terrible job, but somebody has to do it. The flagged reviews are pouring in to the Goodreads office. The ones in the overflowing in-tray arrived while he was having a ten minute coffee break. (He'll need something stronger than coffee soon.)

The thing is, what does he do with this beautifully argued review here by Manny, which is all about the terrible Holocaust denier David Irving, or my own huffy denunciation of the homophobic Orson Scott Card's opinions?

These clearly should be zapped. We say loudly that we're not going to read these books and the authors are awful.

The New GR Policy was thought up to try to cool things out over there in the YA section, where reviewers and authors have at times, I regret to say, indulged in unseemly name-calling. But there is such a thing as logic and fairness.

So if any reviews have been deleted entirely from GR, the above two should by the same rule.

I will be posting a copy of this short introduction to Logic to the GR head office in San Francisco. It might help.

A Review of "Tampa"

I'm really confused about what I can write and what I can't write here on Goodreads. One of my recent reviews was deleted for being not about the book.

> Your review of Logic: A Very Short Introduction *was recently flagged by Goodreads members as potentially off-topic. As the review is not about the book, it has been removed from the site.*

I can't complain about that, they were quite right — I had actually put that book on my TO READ shelf, so by definition, I hadn't read it yet.

So the logic is, I think, that ANY remark about a book you haven't read yet is "potentially off-topic".

This means that ANY comments you have made about a book on your TO READ shelves should be deleted by the unhappy staff members who are tasked with zapping this stuff. (Do they read George Orwell essays in their lunch breaks? I would like to think so.)

They don't need to wait for the non-review to be flagged, they can just go ahead and zap any review they find on anyone's TO READ shelf. But, you know, they aren't doing that ... so far. Well, not to me, anyway.

So until we get a little more clarity about this, I would like to present a short entertainment which I freely admit cannot possibly be a review of *Tampa* because I haven't read it yet, and therefore is "potentially off-topic".

Okay, enough with the mealymouth, I'll make it simple: it's COMPLETELY off-topic. There you go, I'm trying to help here.

HOW TO CHOOSE YOUR NEXT NOVEL

When I'm three quarters through my current novel I get the urge to pick the next one. It's a horrible urge — next, next, next. O the disease of novel-reading — one ailment I hope I'm never cured of. So anyway, which one to choose out of the dozens on the groaning shelf? The one with the sexiest cover? The one with the waggly tail? No, that's how you choose which dog to buy. How about the serious one which has been sitting glowering at me for about a decade and which will make me a better person?

So I thought I'd approach the problem scientifically this time, and base my decision on First Lines. I mean, if I was a novelist, I'd want to spear the reader like a fish with a really strong first line. So I'm the fish, spear me.

Here are ten contenders, taken from the groaning shelf at random.

1. *Tampa* by Alissa Nutting

   I spent the night before my first day of teaching in an excited loop of hushed masturbation on my side of the mattress, never falling asleep.

   Wow, like not sleeping for the whole night? Wouldn't you be totally zombified on your first day at the new job? Anyway, yeah, I want to know what kind of nutcase we're dealing with here, so I'm hooked. 9/10.

2. *Platform* by Michel Houellebecq

   Father died last year.

   Oh that's so tiny I will allow him another sentence.

   I don't subscribe to the theory by which we only become truly adult when our parents die; we never become truly adult.

   Mmm, so so. I can't say I'm bothered one way or the other. 3/10.

3. *The Lowland* by Jhumpa Lahiri

   East of the Tolly Club, after Deshapran Sashmal Road splits in two, there is a small mosque.

   I read a book about literary devices and one chapter was about first lines of novels and the guy was saying that you really need a strong first line, obviously, and he was reeling off all these great ones, you know, Call me Fishmeal and The clocks were striking 13 and all of those. Well, it seems most novelists do not subscribe to this idea at all and are happy to write very dull first sentences. 3/10.

4. *The Mosquito Coast* by Paul Theroux

   We drove past Tiny Polski's mansion house to the main road, and then the five miles into Northampton, Father talking the whole way about savages and the awfulness of America — how it got turned into a dope-taking, door-locking, ulcerated danger-zone of rabid scavengers and criminal millionaires and moral sneaks.

   Yes, that's more like it. I'm interested. Let's go. 7/10.

5. *Continental Drift* by Russell Banks

   It's not memory you need for telling this story, the sad story of Robert Raymond Dubois, the story that ends along the back streets and alleys of Miami, Florida, on a February morning in 1981 ...

   Hold on there, Russell! I finally found a full stop towards the end of page one, it's one of those clausally incontinent whoppers. But yeah, I like that. 7/10.

6. *Burr* by Gore Vidal

   Shortly before midnight, July 1, 1833, Colonel Aaron Burr, aged seventy-seven, married Eliza Jumel, born Bowen fifty-eight years ago (more likely sixty-five but remember: she is prone to litigation!).

Well, this is lighthearted enough. He's trying to put me at ease — this will be history with its tie loosened. Gets its jauntiness in immediately. Nice. 8/10

7. *A Fire Upon the Deep* by Vernor Vinge

   How to explain? How to describe? Even the omniscient viewpoint quails.

   Oh deario. This is a much-praised space-opera but is that not one of the clunkient, least appetising first lines you've ever seen? Quails? Who says quails? is this going to be a novel where they use verily and quoth? Back on the shelf. 0 out of 10.

8. *Omensetter's Luck* by William H. Gass

   Now folks today we're going to auction off Missuss Pimber's things.

   I love this, I instantly want to read on. There's no quotation marks, this being The Gassman, a notorious modernist, so I'm expecting it to be all streamily conscious and that. 8/10.

9. *Crystal Vision* by Gilbert Sorrentino

   I will call this drink the Flowers of Summer, the Magician says,

   I would call a drink the Flowers of Summer too, but I hate magicians. 5/10.

10. *Blonde* by Joyce Carol Oates

    There came Death hurtling along the Boulevard in waning sepia light.

    Ooh, that's a bit pulpy and lurid. It's not all going to be like that is it? This is supposed to be about Marilyn Monroe, and she did die. Must be one of those stories that start at the end and then flashback (for 738 pages). 6/10.

So, we have a winner. Alissa, it's you, you saucy minx.

A Philosophical Discussion

[Simon Evnine is a professor of philosophy who, among other things, has published a book about the nature of rationality. His approach to the Goodreads censorship debate has been characteristically logical. It included the following review of Manny Rayner's 2006 book Putting Linguistics into Speech Recognition: The Regulus Grammar Compiler, *published by the University of Chicago Press.]*

SIMON: Despite the fact that this is in my Read shelf, I have never read this book. But I want to talk about its author, Manny Rayner. Manny is one of the greatest people I have ever known. I know for a fact that once, as he was walking in a poor part of the city, he passed a homeless man who was evidently suffering from the DTs. Manny sat with this man, on the filthy, piss-stinking scrub under a bridge, for seven (7) hours, cradling the unfortunate's head in his arms, until the fit passed. Afterwards, the man wept and tried to press into Manny's hands a few grubby coins, which needless to say Manny would not accept.

So no, I haven't read *Putting Linguistics into Speech Recognition: The Regulus Grammar Compiler*, but how could any book about the Regulus Grammar Compiler fail to be wonderful, written by an author with Manny's heaven-drunk soul?

[Simon's review prompted the following exchange with the author, which appeared soon after in the comment thread.]

MANNY: Simon, I had completely forgotten about the incident until you reminded me. I just don't think that kind of thing is a big deal, you understand. In fact, I was about to say it had never happened, when I remembered the detail with the coins. Most panhandlers keep their change clean for some reason (I have never understood why), but this guy was an exception.

PS It is obvious at a glance that you read too many books on logic. Are you sure that's still allowed?

SIMON: Manny, just like you to have forgotten something most of us would be boasting of for our entire lives. "Mensch," "gentleman," "megalopsychia," "kalos k'agathos." These epithets are the best, the noblest I have at my command, and all fall woefully short for you.

As for the logic, I thought my strategy here was a promising one. I may post more under Authors-Behaving-Fantastically.

MANNY: Ah, I'm starting to feel embarrassed. But I'm also a sucker for multilingual compliments, so please feel free to continue.

You are splendidly logical. Anyone would think you were a professor of philosophy or something.

[Twelve hours later, Manny flagged the review.]

MANNY: Like Jacob and the angel, I have wrestled all night with my conscience concerning this review. I must concede. Flattering though it is, and much as I enjoyed the compliments showered on me, none of them are true. The incident Simon describes, quite simply, never took place. My responses were also fabricated, and constituted a desperate attempt to lend substance to Simon's mendacious claims. I retract them now.

This review should be forthwith deleted, as should the shelf that Simon used. If it is inappropriate to use negative shelf names and make hatefully untrue claims about authors in reviews, it surely follows that it is also inappropriate to use positive shelf names and post exaggeratedly laudatory comments on them. There is no reasonable doubt that this review contravenes the current guidelines.

Strike it down! And strike down all similar ones as well. I know very well that this is not the only example of its pernicious breed. They must all be uprooted, all, without mercy, down to the very last comma and animated GIF.

[At publication time, the review had still not been deleted by the Goodreads administrators.]

A Review of "Editorial" by its author

Arthur Graham is a panty-sniffing, booze-hounding, tax-dodging rapscallion, and he has been known to trick people of indeterminate age into viewing nude photos of himself online. He once killed a drifter in order to obtain an erection, and when that failed to work a second time, he started killing kittens instead.

He doesn't love his mother, and he only cleans his toilet once every several months.

Arthur Graham is actually a double-agent working for STGRB, and he is only posting items in protest of GR censorship policies in order to collect "likes" from persons of interest to Michelle Obama and the NSA.

— From Arthur Graham's review of *Editorial*, by Arthur Graham

---

The author continued to bully himself unmercifully in the comment thread, encouraging passers-by to join in. Before long, he had assembled an impressive mob, who had fun flinging abuse at him for several days. Other people flagged this behavior, which blatantly contravened the Terms of Use.

As we go to press, the review has still not been deleted.

A Review of "Martial Law"

The following review is compliant with the new Goodreads ToU

This book is irrelevant to Goodreads because you can't buy it on Amazon. Also it talks about oppression, censorship etc. and no one really likes reading about that because it's boring. Yet, let me tell you anyway.

The title of this book is 'The Image of Everyday Life in Press during the Martial Law', which is a little bit ridiculous because what could be read in Press those days when it was so heavily censored? Well, you had to read between the lines.

The Martial Law was one of the darkest periods of recent Polish history. In December 1981, General Jaruzelski decided he had enough of strikes, protests and demonstrations, and introduced the so called 'Martial Law'. Back then Poland was, funnily enough, called the People's Republic of Poland but it didn't really care about its people. It didn't have to answer to its people. Poland was then only a satellite to the USSR and it only had to answer to Moscow Kremlin. Nowadays, Jaruzelski claims he did what he had to because the USSR was pressuring him and threatening with military action. But unless Russia opens up their archives we will never know if Jaruzelski was just over-zealous in oppressing his country or whether he was just following orders from the USSR.

Martial Law started before anyone knew what was happening. Overnight they arrested thousands of people, turned off the phones, and closed the borders. And then they announced there would be new laws. New laws, which were arbitrary and often frankly puzzling. Sometimes you wouldn't know about things that were banned until you got in trouble. It was almost as if they were making them up as they went on. There was a curfew (at different times in different cities), a ban on travelling outside your town, a ban on public assembly, there was even a ban on most water sports (and no one knew why that was). Once the phones were turned back on, all the conversations were monitored, and you could be arrested or even forced out of the country if you were caught saying something the government didn't like.

So what did people do? How could they rebel against the oppression when the other side had tanks, tear gas, riot teams and a whole of USSR? And yet they did. When the 8 o'clock news came on (censored and full of propaganda), they left their houses and went for walks. They would greet all their neighbours and keep walking, just so they are not accused of public assembly. The government's response was to push the curfew, so that everyone had to stay at home for the evening news. The people would wear the Solidarity Movement symbols, but those were soon banned (together with all other political symbols), so people started pinning 'resistors' to their jackets. A resistor is just an electrical component, it cannot possibly be described as a political symbol. It's just a piece of metal, and yet there it was. A tiny little sign of resistance.

The cultural events were banned and there was strict censorship. But what's censorship to people who had been dealing with communism for forty years? They knew how to play that game. They knew how to write about what they wanted to write about, pretending they were writing about, say, the Spanish Inquisition, but it really was about the here and now. And their audience knew that and they winked at the artist, and the artist winked back at them. And even the government knew it but they couldn't do anything, unless they admitted they were in fact acting like the Spanish Inquisition. Some say that Polish artists have never been as creative as in those days. That the opposition had liberated a certain energy in them, some sense of a true mission.

During Martial Law lots of Polish people emigrated, not because they wanted to. They loved Poland but they just could not function in that reality. Some people were forced to emigrate, they got a one way ticket and were banned from returning. Many stayed and fought. Some openly and bravely (in a way sure to get them in trouble), some in a more quiet and symbolic way. Others did nothing, they just tried to go about their lives and navigate somehow this new reality. Yet, some said it didn't affect them, they said you wouldn't have anything to worry about if you were a law-abiding citizen. They even sent letters to newspapers thanking the government for bringing peace and order and shutting down the troublemakers. Some say it was the government themselves sending those letters.

Did any of those little rebellious acts work? Many people said: why bother, why bother wearing a metal resistor in your jacket? How are you going to win against the USSR and their army with a resistor in your jacket. Don't fool yourself, you're not running against the Polish government, the Polish government has no say in what is happening in Poland, because Poland is fully owned by the USSR. You can't win, you can't beat the USSR. I guess, if you stopped and thought about it, you would realise it was true, which is why you didn't stop to think about it. You just kept on with the resistor in your jacket. And a few years later, what do you know ... the Solidarity movement which started in Poland spread to other countries and the Iron Curtain crumbled. And maybe the Soviet Block was doomed to fail, maybe it was all the geopolitical and economic factors, but who can say it wasn't the resistor in your jacket?

(licensed by oomlout under CC-BY-SA 2.0 Generic:
http://commons.wikimedia.org/wiki/File:220_ohms_5\%25_axial_resistor.jpg)

A Review of "The Master and Margarita"

At the hour of the brisk fall sunrise, two citizens appeared at the Boston Commons. One of them, a man of about forty, with hunched shoulders under an astrakhan coat, was short, black-haired, and moony-eyed beneath tortoise-shell spectacles. The other, younger, maybe early-twenties, tall and thin, in a red tartan and blue-jeans, tousled chestnut-hair, and sleepy lashes, was looking out over the greying gardens. For some reason this younger citizen was fingering something in his pocket, devil knows what.

The first was none other than Mikhail Mikhailovich Kuklov, a slick editor for the local Arts and Culture Journal for the city, and anyway a chairman of the board at the Theatre and at the Public Library, his young companion was a book-reviewer named David Davidovich Davidov, who wrote under the pseudonym of Listless.

They were crossing through the gardens, toward the cold-glassy pond, wherein floated the lifeless chassis of the city's famous cygnet-skiffs. Passing the lifeless swans and crossing a small stone footbridge, they dashed first-thing to the lone, bright sign of a hot-bun vendor reading "Hot Boston Buns: $5.00." A steep price for buns, anyway.

It should be noted at this point a most peculiar feature of this dreary October morning. There was not one person, neither ten people, but precisely no one in the park, save for our two high-minded citizens at the bun stand. There was no one in the Commons, not up on the monument hill, nor down in the field, nor on the cement-grey paths: not one person. It was the same story in the Gardens: not one person by the pond, nor by the fountains, nor walking the criss-cross gardened ways. No one!

— "Two coffees," Kuklov asked.
— "No coffee, mister," replied the bun vendor.
— "Tea, then?"
— "No tea, neither."

— "So what do you have? Something warm for the stomach?" Kuklov asked, anyway, annoyed.

— "...Buns, mister. Or hot cocoa," the merchant rejoined, also, for some reason, annoyed, though he had no other customers to speak of.

— "The cocoa then," David Davidovich cut in.

The vendor poured two white Styrofoam cups precisely three-quarters of the way with the molten cocoa, which sent streamers of steam curling in the morning air. Having hazarded a sip, Kuklov confirmed his suspicion that the hot beverage was, in fact, too hot, and having confirmed this walked with his companion adroitly to the park bench beside the rental nest for the swan-shaped sloops, floating lifeless on the still water.

David looked around anxiously. Large abandoned parks made him anxious for some reason. Perhaps it had something to do with what psychologists called precisely agoraphobia, or perhaps it was just a vague apprehension for the unmet potential for so vast a space. He etiolated and turned toward the bridge, thinking: "what is wrong with me ... I must be cracked to be so nervous, for no reason! Maybe it's time, anyway, to send it to the devil and pack it up for ..." This thought was disrupted presently by his older companion who let out an idle sigh, which was for some reason very disruptive.

David was thinking about his column. He had recently read Bulgakov's *The Master and Margarita* for the Massachusetts Literary Journal, Masslit for short, which was precisely the same Journal for which his friend was the esteemed editor. It was about the forty-sixth anniversary of its publication, which seemed a strange anniversary to celebrate, thought David, but he had received his orders and written his review, anyway. The talking cat had seemed a bit of a trite invention to him, but he wrote a nice review anyway, for some reason, and when it was done he had liked it.

All of a sudden, to the editor's displeasure, there appeared in the road a very tall woman, taller than he had ever seen, but for some reason, seeming to disappear in air, pellucid like water in the air before him. And where did she come from? I couldn't say, and neither, for that matter could Mikhail Mikhailovich. She wore a long yellow sundress with white-wisps of floral-arabesques, very unseasonable, but for some reason she didn't look cold at all! She shimmered in the air briefly before him, and when he blinked, she was gone precisely from the spot she had just occupied on the pavement. He blinked twice quickly, like a facial tick-tick, to check himself doubly, and looked at his fellow citizen to glean his companion's corresponding reaction, but David seemed not to have noticed for some reason, so he dismissed the strange Amazon, which anyway seemed to him an amazing apparition of great power and strange beauty.

"Pah! the devil!" exclaimed the editor. "I must've had a stroke or something! I thought I saw some seven-foot Amazon in a damned yellow dress, for a second, do you believe it? Some kind of Hippolyta-broad! Seven feet, by god, and shimmering like a hologram! My god, this cocoa has gone straight to my head" (or anyway to his waist). David looked at him, a bit disturbed, but mostly in disbelief. He let some time pass and for the strange occurrence to ebb away. "Your review, you know, David. It was no good."

— "What, Mik? What was bad about it?"
— "Well if I am being honest, it was a bit off-topic, y'know? All those damned bits about revolutions and history and your personal bullshit, yeah, those trite personal bits, those really were a bit off, y'know Dave?"
— "It's a personal review style, I've always written like that, Mik . . . have the readership complained or something?"
— "No that's not it, Dave, and you know I love your reviews, man, really I do." Mikhail Mikhailovich responded warmly. He explained that it was new management of some kind. Anyway the Masslit Journal had been bought out, devil knows why, by precisely some big corporate bulldog-type. And despairing though he was, and dreading the changes that would come, David Davidovich's despair was cut short by the appearance of a strange, foreign looking man.

— "Hey Mik, looks like the park isn't empty anyway, look at that odd fellow!" David said.
— "He must be from the South, Georgia or something, look at those damned-unusual clothes!" he conjectured, for the odd man was wearing a light spring coat and khakis (too short), my god, he was wearing short khaki pants, and you could see his lozenged silk socks, clashing quite horribly with his Oxford wingtips and damned strange thick horn-rimmed glasses.
— "Yea, and those specs! Georgia, maybe, or Europe maybe, somewhere in France? Those French fellows are damned odd." Mikhail Mikhailovich agreed, and posited that maybe somewhere Nordic, or in the Eastern block: Poland, the Czech Republic, Russia even, maybe! But before they could quite come to a consensus on the strange foreigner's origins, he had approached them, and began:
— "Were you talking, just now, about Bulgakov?"
The two citizens literally jumped with surprise and their nape-hairs bristled in their jackets at the bell-clear English of their odd interlocutor. For some reason, and by some how, they were both certain that he was precisely a foreigner, but also that he was precisely a native.
— " ...yes, citizen, we were." David replied after the intercession of what seemed maybe too long to be polite.
— "Excellent, excellent novelist, you think? That devil and his great goetic tricks! Such fun, eh?"
At this, they suspected he might be Canadian, but anyway, they couldn't be precisely sure. David pushed his ears back and down into his shoulder and gestured a small shrug of tepid agreement, and was accompanied by his companion with a dubious nod. — "And that Pontius Pilate, what a damned character, eh? All that red-lined white robed procurator and his damned sentimentality and half-baked conviction for that pretty pious Ha-Nozri, pah! To the devil with him!" And with this last comment he looked down the lane at a barren oak and then shot a sly stare at this benched acquaintances, askance, as if to check boiling water.
— "Yes, yes, very interesting. Excellent piece of fiction, timeless."

the editor said, to appease the strange man.

— "Fiction? But my friend, every word of it is precisely true! Yes, yes, the whole thing, the master, and the sanatorium, and lovely Queen Margot, and Woland, yes, Woland and his retinue! The whole thing, really. Do you believe it? Yes, every word."

At this, the two citizens looked at each other, and for some reason could literally read each other's minds. And it was that they were talking precisely to a madman, and that for some reason it felt eerily familiar, though they could not pin down just why that was.

From the corners of their eyes they observed a tall woman in a knee-length brown coat, with sheer lining, and boots to match, with a small girl in similar dress, but with a woolen purple hat and red mittens, at the bun stand. The mother bought her and her daughter buns, and bit into them with a womanly savoir-faire. David thought for some reason that this woman, instead of relieving his apprehension of the empty park, heightened it by accentuating the emptiness, and the innocent young daughter seemed a daisy-bud exposed to the bitter frost of a wide-open windowsill. He was watching them walk away, when the strange foreigner, who must have followed his gaze, asked him adroitly: "Youth! Ah, but alas sometimes it ends too soon, don't you think, David Davidovich?"

Precisely shocked, David Davidovich asked, "How do you know my name?" — "From your reviews of course! Listless ... David Davidovich, yes, it would seem your pseudonym is not as effective when you are proudly credited in the back fold, eh? But like I said, it is sad for youth to end so soon, eh — like that precious girl over there, pretty as a porcelain doll, but alas! as fragile."

— "What do you mean?" David asked apprehensively, for this thought had occurred to him a lot recently. People had been disappearing lately in quite strange circumstances. Yes, strange circumstances, strange precisely because they were completely unexplained! And not only youths, but his coevals also, his contemporaries. Authors, co-workers, landlords, police-officers and traffic cops, the barista at the coffee shop beneath his apartment, and strangely even the woman he had been seeing (for two dinners and a breakfast, anyway), had disappeared like smoke in the wind, like water in water. One day they were there in front of him: comforting familiar faces, the next day they were disconnected phone lines, or vacant subway seats, or vague, veiled "they're not in today"s, all over the city! Suddenly his heart pulled up in his chest, and he felt like he would eat it. That poor girl! He felt for some reason that she too would disappear.

— "Why, because she is going to die today, I'm afraid," the strange foreigner said with what could have been genuine or mock sentiments.

From the top of his throat, David's heart dropped suddenly to the pit of his stomach, pulling down into his bowels with a stunned sort of fear. He felt unable to speak.

— "Nonsense, nonsense!" Kuklov said, after his long silence and nervous stillness. He was certain now that he was talking to a madman, a complete madman!

— "Ah, Mikhail Mikhailovich! I had nearly forgotten you were here, and to think! With so much of you to forget!" he said, looking at his corpulent companion folded fat-wise on the bench. Kuklov demurred. "But enough of that sad business, I should introduce myself, how impolite of me!"

The two citizens, literally reeling from the pronounced death-knell of the young girl who was sprightly walking away now with her mother, had to admit they had been curious of the identity of their interlocutor. Though, they were still in shock.

— "Jeff Wilke," he said with veiled pride.

The two stunned citizens looked at each other. Neither recognized the name.

— "You're thinking 'who is this Wilke fellow? Like we should know him by name, damned bastard!' — am I correct? Well anyway, I work for A——" he replied with oracular clarity and precision.

Mikhail Mikhailovich felt a brief black haze of syncope, jumped up, and was suddenly out of breath. It should be noted now that the

Masslit Journal, a regional journal of the Goodreads Community, Inc. (a national Art & Culture magazine, printed under a wide variety of regional standards) had been purchased by this very same A—— company! This very same! And it was precisely this change in management which had necessitated this conversation with the young Listless. He felt his heart humming louder and faster, clanging in his chest like a hammer on steel. He looked first at David, and then at this strange Mr. Wilke. His heart throbbed with indecision and uncertainty, and he felt he would die ...

With still tepid indecision, he extended his hand, not knowing precisely was he was doing, and said "Nice ... to me– ... et you ..."

— "To the devil with it!" the editor thought, when this strange Mr. Wilkes took his hand with enthusiasm and with a strange stare which seemed to see past Mikhail Mikhailovich, seemed to see through him.

David still sat, not knowing precisely what happened, having not heard the details of A——, though of course he know of it vaguely, like a lighthouse in the fog. But before he could get up and do the same as his deferential editor, he heard a Hellish clamor!

Behind them, there was screaming and smoke, and people pouring about like water from a broken bucket. The air was still with white noise and a hollow vibration of horror, as the grey nightmare was uncovered and pieced together with jigsaw terror. A sleepy driver had hit the young girl, and she had been precisely decapitated by the veritable vehicle of death! A thick-red ooze pooled in the street, and the mother was prostrate in sorrow on the sidewalk, being fanned by a pedestrian. Where this pedestrian and all these witnesses came from, devil knows! When David returned to himself, which may have taken minutes, or precisely even tens of minutes, he didn't know. He was surprised to see that the mysterious Mr. Wilke had gone! Disappeared! And even stranger still, so had Mikhail Mikhailovich! Where had they gone? He would never know! He looked again towards the accident, to see if in the confusion they had hurried to the girl's or the mother's aid, but they were not there! "To the devil with them!" he thought.

After a minute or so, he stood up on still uncertain legs, and started to walk home to his small studio apartment, where he supposed he would call Mikhail Mikhailovich, and also maybe begin to re-tool his review of Bulgakov's *The Master and Margarita* — which he for some reason remembered now, even though his brain was literally swimming with the foggy phantoms of that morning. And foggy too! The late morning had brought on a strange fog! "By god, what a strange morning" he thought, walking through the billowing sheets of the foggy October day. For it was no longer morning, it was precisely eleven, and he had to go home.

And the fog seemed to get thicker, and he wondered where the devil could Kuklov have gone, and why the devil he had left. And then looking around he wondered where the devil *he* was. And for some reason he was never seen again.

A Review of "Drive"

The End is Much More Exciting than It Was Once Upon a Time

The story of GoodBetterBestReads has really only just begun, but we have already become the world's largest community of potential readers, book buyers and Kindle users who have star-rated a book at least once in the last 12 months.

The problem is you can't buy a condo or a beer off the back of potential alone. We need people to buy books, and to do that we need people who can sell books.

That's where you come in.

If you were ever interested in reading, writing, reviewing, we want to speak to you. We want you on our team.

We could harness your skills and change your mindset for ever. We could help you exchange old passions for new.

Ever wanted to turn your passion into a career? Easy. We could help you transition from your love of books to a love of sales.

The Importance of Sales

Look at it this way. There are so many books available now, it would be a crime not to try to sell them.

There's nothing we've got that we can't sell. Without a little help from you.

We love books, but let's face it, we love them even more when they're at your place.

So we need you to find a home for every book we could possibly think of selling.

And guess what, we're totally format-neutral. Tree books, we've got warehouses. E-books, we've got cyberspace. But to be honest, if we could shift more e-books, our staff wouldn't have to work in smelly warehouses. Think about it. Our staff come first.

The Next Chapter

Do you know what the biggest problem about a community is?

The 80/20 rule? Heard of that? It's worse in cyberspace. Let us tell you. You won't believe this. 99% of reviews on GoodBetterBestReads are written by less than one percent of the members.

Did you hear that? 99%! Let's repeat it. 99%. Let's repeat it. 99%.

Now, the thing is, we thought that by getting one percent to do all the writing, we could sell to the 100%.

We placed a lot of trust in the one percent. Can you see our dilemma? A lot of people's welfare depended on the one percent.

What would happen to our cocktails and our cars and our condos, if the one percent staged a strike? Exactly, you know what I mean. You probably feel the same about your job. VULNERABLE!!! Let's repeat it. VULNERABLE!!!

And You Thought You Knew What a Staff Review Was!

Let's be totally honest with you. Our original business model was flawed. It was too highly dependent on community. There is only so long that the one percent will carry the 99%. And it's not long. It's unsustainable. Especially if your exit strategy is a sale to an online bookseller.

I suppose we could have encouraged the 99% to do more selling. But honestly, what we really want them to do is more buying.

So, guess what, we decided to approach the problem a different way.

What if we could reduce our dependence on the one percent? What if less people, not more, could write all of the reviews?

So now we're going to get our staff to write the reviews. It's so brilliant, it's a wonder we didn't think of it earlier.

This is our opportunity to talk about you.

If you're bright ... If you're talented ... If you love books ... If you love writing ... If you love reviewing ... don't worry, it doesn't matter.

We just need you to punch out reviews.

Our mission is to help people find and buy books they love. If that's your kind of story, let's do business.

Our goal: Two million staff reviews in three years!

Just think, you could write 30,000 of them!

Personal, Political, Cultural: Parsing the Concept of Author Behavior in Goodreads Policy

Late last week [on Friday September 20], Goodreads announced a new "policy change". The announcement opened with a reiteration of policy points regarding reviews which haven't changed: reviews should be about the book, and members cannot threaten other members. This is what had changed:

> [Goodreads will] Delete content focused on author behavior. We have had a policy of removing reviews that were created primarily to talk about author behavior from the community book page. Once removed, these reviews would remain on the member's profile. Starting today, we will now delete these entirely from the site. We will also delete shelves and lists of books on Goodreads that are focused on author behavior.

Previously, the policy had been that reviews that spoke negatively about author behavior — *I will not read this book because something the author said or did* — were removed from the main book page, but were still visible to friends. For those that don't use Goodreads, if you look up a book, all your friends' reviews are listed first, then those by people you follow, then the "community reviews". This last category was where your review would not show up. This policy of hiding reviews I thought was a fair one: one that maintained the social aspects of the site, as users could signal to one another that they weren't going to read something, and why, while muffling the effects of these peer-to-peer interactions on the larger community.

But Goodreads didn't go through and just delete all hidden reviews, nor did they remove all shelves entitled "due-to-author" or similar. In this "policy change", Goodreads instead removed the shelves and some reviews of 21 specific people. As far as I can tell, everyone else's hidden reviews are still standing, and Goodreads spokesperson Kara indicated on the feedback thread that it wasn't just the shelf names, but, like, the general feel of the reviews under that shelf header? Which, frankly, looks seriously personal and isn't so much a policy change as swatting specific users, especially given the tone of the email they received.

> Please refrain from posting content like this going forward. If you continue to act in a way that is contrary to the spirit and intent of Goodreads, your account will come under review.

Admittedly, Goodreads has apologized for not giving users time to edit, because alerting people to major deletions and then acting like people should have magically known the policy would change and were violating it on purpose is bunk.

This is the problem: if the reviews in question were all "this person was a dick to me on Twitter/Goodreads/etc", then I can see Goodreads justifying their removal under the already existing guideline that you can't say the author owes you money or whatnot. That could be construed as a personal interaction, and therefore not germane. This is a little complicated by the fact that Goodreads and Twitter are public, and the interactions become a matter of record. (At least until they don't, as these sorts of interaction tend to get deleted.) But, okay, let's just call them personal interactions, and say that kind of interaction is off the table, and always has been. No need for a policy change, as it's just a policy refinement. The personal behavior — in the sense of person to person interactions — of an author amounts to gossip, maybe, fine.

But I'm a little more worried about what I see as creep in the policy towards silencing *political* responses or *cultural* responses based on the author's actions or words. Self-avowedly, Mike's review of *Mein Kampf* is a troll, because of course it's stupid to say that you can't mention that *Adolf freaking Hitler* was a genocidal maniac.

That's a matter of the historical record, and unassailable. And in fact, when you deny Hitler's actions, you can go to jail for it in some countries. Manny took the troll a step further in his review of *The Destruction of Dresden* by David Irving, who was convicted of Holocaust denial in Austria. (The Austrians have, historically understandably, harsher rules about this sort of speech there than in the US.) Irving's behavior isn't gossip or personal; it's a matter of political record. Knowing that he is a Holocaust denier in a history book about the Holocaust is absolutely germane to that content.

Kemper's review of *Josey Wales: Two Westerns* is also about the author's political actions. Asa Earl Carter (who wrote under several pen-names) was a longtime member of the KKK and one of two men credited with the "segregation now, segregation forever" speech by George Wallace. The choice not to read the works of vociferous racists in your precious leisure time isn't some kind of readerly tantrum, and if it were, what's it to you? Trigger warning: Asa Earl Carter was insanely racist. That has serious import on his work.

Arguably, GR could take the tack that these are historical actions, and it's not like the authors are going to be flagging these reviews from the grave (or prison). But let's take Orson Scott Card. (Take Orson Scott Card! Please!) Paul's review notes Card's very active and visible status as an anti-gay crusader. Mr. Card has called for the overthrow of the American government, and worked visibly to pass Prop 8 in California. There are boycott movements all over the place for the upcoming film. Noting this isn't "Card owes me money" or "Card was mean to me on Twitter" but a contextualizing of his work within a political and cultural framework. Orson Scott Card impacts me *politically*. This isn't gossip. This is cultural engagement. *Of course* you don't have to agree. Of course you can compartmentalize Card's political beliefs from his work. But the refusal to read Card *as a political act* is valid too, and it's a political act that cannot occur without knowledge of the larger context, context provided by reviews such as Paul's.

I have also taken several swipes at serial plagiarist Jonah Lehrer, in defiance of the new "policy". The first review was of *How We Decide*, one of two of his books that were recalled by the publisher for fabrication and/or plagiarism. Drat, I thought, that the book was recalled for its content is actually about the content. So I posted on his only unrecalled book, *Proust Was a Neuroscientist*. But *this is still about context*. Lehrer has just an appalling track record of unprofessional behavior — behavior that has gotten him fired from multiple science writing gigs — and this behavior calls into question any science writing this man has done. He wasn't mean to me on Twitter, he fudged data, which in a science writer in inexcusable. I guess I could append the namby-pamby "to me", like science writing is about *opinions*, but I'm not going to. He violated the basic tenets of the subject he was writing about.

But let's take this a step down, away from the political or professional. One of the reviews deleted under the new policy was Steph Sinclair's for *The Secret of Castle Cant: Being an Account of the Remarkable Adventures of Lucy Wickwright, Maidservant and Spy*. The author, K.P. Bath, was convicted of possession of child pornography and sentenced to six years in prison, which is also a matter of record. It is germane to a review of his children's book that he is a convicted pedophile. To quote U.S. Attorney Dwight Holton:

> "It is shocking that a children's author would contribute to the trauma these kids endure — both physical and emotional trauma from the sexual abuse itself, and psychological trauma from knowing that images of that abuse are circulating on the Internet."

This is not gossip. Multiple reviews still left on Goodreads note this fact and literally nothing else about the book. I reviewed Jerry Sandusky's book and noted his conviction on 45 counts of child abuse, and I'm not the only one. They are all still standing, because it is patently ridiculous to say that Sandusky's conviction doesn't have a bearing on the content of his self-elegy about how great he was to kids, or that Bath's pedophilia doesn't factor into his children's book. That there are many, many reviews still standing that note these facts makes me wonder what the sandwich is going on with this new policy.

It's looking to me that Goodreads is swatting very specific users, and backing it up with confusing, badly considered "policy changes" that aren't so much changes as after-the-fact justifications. Out of a site of millions of users, that Goodreads went after 21 people looks underhanded and sneaky. That Goodreads cannot with clarity articulate what exactly the policy is — it's not shelf names, or maybe it is; of course you can talk about the author, unless you can't — is an indicator that it's not a policy change but policy incoherence.

These deletions ended up being a signal to users that Goodreads is changing its focus from community development to marketing to authors. Amazon acquired Goodreads last year, and I think this is the signal that things are going to change to a more business friendly site. There have always been important differences in Amazon and Goodreads reviews: Goodreads allows profanity, for example, because it's not a store, but a social network. (The Terms of Use, like most social networking sites, specifically disallows users under the age of 13, so you don't have to think of the children.) There has never been a downvoting system on Goodreads either, because it really doesn't matter if the review is "helpful" to every user; it has not been about sales. While I've been reluctant to engage in paranoid tin-foil-hattery about how Amazon was going to ruin everything, it is not mouth-frothing to note that Amazon has to make their money somehow, and I can tell you it's not necessarily going to be through book sales, but the marketing dollars of authors.

In this interview by Community Manager Patrick Brown about Goodreads uploaded in August, he focuses largely on the utility of Goodreads to authors, explaining their recommendation algorithm and discussing how the social networking aspects fuel the discovery process. (Discovery being the buzzword these days about how writers go about getting a book into the hands of readers, as the traditional publishing model splinters and bursts into flames.) Reviews that focus on author behavior — and of course we are not children, so we know this means negative reviews that focus on author behavior — are disruptive to the discovery process from the point of view of the author: you are hearing about my book all wrong!

So, so many of the writings I see out there discussing this policy change note the recent allegations of a young woman who claimed to have been bullied on Goodreads. Salon asks:[14] Did a writer get bullied on Goodreads? They repeat her initial claims that her book was tagged with shelves titled "author should be sodomized" and "should be raped in prison". The link to her Tweets, which was the only evidence of this claim, goes to a deleted page, and there was never a link to any Goodreads shelves, because they *never existed*. (Here we get into the issue of why a self-referenced post on Twitter isn't a credible source, for those paying attention, **journalists**.)

If you actually bother to read to the end of the article, there's a lame ETA noting that that she eventually issued an "LOL, my bad", admitting she misunderstood pretty much everything about Goodreads reviewing culture, the shelving system, and that *the rape and death threats had never occurred*. If you want an extremely thorough accounting of the timeline of events, check this post on ThreeRs,[15] which documents copiously what exactly happened.

The damage had been done at this point, unfortunately, because in this brave new journalistic world that drives blog-arms of media outlets to half-ass their sources in order to get pages up fast while the controversy is breaking — page views! (I'm assuming things here about Goodreads's motivation, but I can't really figure why they'd kick this hornet's nest so hard if they weren't attempting to appear "tough on bullying" or something. Especially factoring in the recent

---

[14] http://www.salon.com/2013/08/21/debut_author_allegedly_got_rape_threats_on_goodreads/

[15] http://threears.wordpress.com/2013/08/29/lauren-pippahoward-throws-a-tantrum-the-internet-falls-all-over-itself-to-give-her-candy-bike-still-on-order/

rape threat meltdown on Twitter.) In this sloppy, bloggy new journalism, you get articles like this one on CNN, which credulously reiterates the fiction that an author had been bullied on Goodreads ZOMG, citing the Salon article, ignoring the retraction, and anemically noting that:

> It's hard to corroborate Howard's story when she's deleted her Tumblr (it's not available in Google's cache) and many of the Goodreads reviews and shelves allegedly devoted to bullying her have also been deleted. In addition, Howard backtracked on some of her statements.

Spoiler alert: you can't corroborate the story because it didn't happen that way at all.

But let's just backtrack. Let's say Howard's books had been shelved in ways that said she should be raped and murdered. This would be horrible and wrong, and it would be right of Goodreads to delete these shelves and ban the users who said such things. I have seen threats on Goodreads — usually users against users and not involving authors at all — and Goodreads has always been good about deleting them once the comments have been flagged. (And sometimes going so far as to ban users.) **The policy in place was already equipped to deal with personal threats**.

Extending the Goodreads Terms of Service to this vague, mushy, overly broad policy about "author behavior" doesn't solve Goodreads's PR problem out there due to bad journalism, irresponsible blog posts, and the fact that people on the Internet can suck. Maybe what they mean is "Twitter isn't a credible source" (actually, no it isn't) or "no more personal interaction stories, even secondhand ones" (ok, that's a shift, but a slighter one than this encompassing "behavior" nonsense.)

Goodreads has been reticent to discuss specific users' deletions, which I guess makes sense in terms of not gossiping in public about users, but in terms of parsing what exactly they are looking for, make it very difficult indeed. Goodreads employee Kara notes:

> Anyone else with reviews or shelves created prior to September 21, 2013 that will be deleted under the revised policy will be sent a notification first and given time to decide what to do.

I take this to mean that reviews not adhering to this vague policy written after the announcement will be deleted without notification. Given that I can't even tell what's actionable anymore, I find this incredibly chilling. Way to turn a PR problem into a firestorm, Goodreads.

The implementation of this policy change has been breathtakingly badly managed, and the thinking behind their shift muzzy and indistinct, when it doesn't look calculated towards aims that have nothing to do with the reviews in question. Goodreads has moved from muffling users to silencing them because they are shifting their focus from peer-to-peer interactions — a social network — to the marketing potentials in a website of 20 million readers. It's been said before, but the user is the product on any social networking site. They can't sell you if you won't behave.

Part IV

Trying to be reasonable

Some members posted pieces trying to analyze what had gone wrong. Arthur, himself a self-published author, argued that the crisis had been caused by oversensitive self-published authors. Manny wrote a review of communication expert Deborah Tannen's *That's Not What I Meant!* in which, following the style of the author, he suggested that the problem was essentially a simple misunderstanding. The review was deleted for being "off-topic".

Goodreads management made no attempt to answer the tens of thousands of queries and comments which were piling up all over the site, beyond posting a brief assurance, in the Feedback area, that their policies did not constitute censorship. This heightened the sense of frustration for people who wanted clarity concerning the new rules that were now being applied.

Goodreads Get Real

As an author, I don't mind telling you that I hardly had any readership to speak of before joining Goodreads. That's one reason why I try to stay active on this site — pure self-interest, I'll admit it. But the main reason why I'm active on Goodreads has nothing to do with selling loads of books or recruiting legions of fans (neither of which have actually happened, btw). Rather, what keeps me coming back are the people — readers and writers alike — who together make this place such a worthwhile online destination to begin with. Sure, every social networking site is gonna have its share of assholes, and I've probably been that asshole at points myself (usually late at night, after too much to drink). But the fact is, if you like to talk about books and you're not a complete moron, you've probably found acceptance here, just like I have. And that's because by and large, Goodreads has always seemed to function like a self-governing anarchy, a big tent where people are allowed to do their thing and speak their minds, even if those things and minds are sometimes total horse shit. Despite minor conflicts, a generally civil ethic has prevailed, perhaps because readers tend to be more intelligent and empathetic on the whole, at least when compared to those illiterate savages on Facebook.

All of this has begun to change recently, and I suppose it all started when some people got a little mean, some people got a little sensitive, and dear old Otis decided to sell the lot of us out to Amazon. All of this has already been covered quite extensively elsewhere, so there's really no point in me weighing in any further than that.

Because of Goodreads, I've experienced both friendship and love, I've had the opportunity to read and be read, and I even got to post a nude photo of myself for a good cause. I'm sure that I'll miss this place dearly if I ever have to leave, and it's because of all you good readers and all your good reads that I've resisted the urge thus far.

Honestly, since this whole thing began, I've vacillated between thinking that readers were being a little paranoid/overdramatic and worrying that maybe they were right, and we really were coming to live under a police state, like so much of the wider "free" world. Now, I'm starting to feel a bit like Martin Niemöller, as more and more of my friends find themselves being censored, exiled, and otherwise rounded up by the Goodreads police.

Frankly, if someone wants to write my book a mean-spirited review, shelve it under "wouldratherchokeonmotoroilspooge", or rate it one star without ever having read a single page, I don't flag this kind of behavior, because it already says much more about the people engaging in it than it does about me or my associates. Not only that, but the day we silence their voices, we've just endorsed our own silencing as well, and the next thing you know, there's no critical thought or community left on Goodreads, either.

That said, I still love this place, as I love all of you — for now, anyway. I guess I'll know it's time to leave when all the real readers/reviewers have flown the coop for warmer climes, and all that's left are a bunch of cold, bitter, flag-happy crybabies.

I guess what I'm really trying to say is that, as an author who's decided to publish his work, I am realistic enough, intelligent enough, and mature enough to understand that not everyone is going to love it, some are going to hate it, and most just won't give a shit. And whatever their reasons, that's their prerogative. If an author gets a lot of bad reviews, or if a reviewer is snarky towards them or their precious baby, it is wrong for them to assume that they are being bullied, and even wronger still for them to demand censorship as a solution, especially when what they should really be doing is honing their craft, fine-tuning their marketing strategy, and just generally getting over themselves already. Then again, I'm that weird author who loves negative reviews, not only because they help to carve out your audience just as well, but also because they can be a golden opportunity for reflection and growth.

In the end, I'm just saddened to know that GR reviews must now be censored, all because every miserable shit on Earth thinks they're a great writer, and no one is allowed to say otherwise.

A Review of "That's Not What I Meant!"

Much as I enjoy childishly flinging dung at the other guys, I wondered whether it might not also be interesting to try and approach the current Goodreads mini-crisis in a constructive way. I don't actually know what's going on, and of course it may be the case that the Goodreads management are taking orders from Amazon, STGRB and our lizard overlords. But let's just for a moment consider the possibility that this could be a breakdown in communication between two essentially well-meaning parties with reasonable goals.

On that admittedly far-fetched hypothesis, one might argue that the Goodreads management basically want not much more than to reserve the right to delete posts which are genuinely dangerous: rape threats, extreme cyberbullying, and similar. The enraged reviewers, similarly, don't want much more than to know that their posts will not be arbitrarily deleted without warning. If this is really what's going on, it's conceivable that we might reach a compromise satisfactory to both sides.

If the Goodreads management only want to be able to remove dangerous posts, it seems to me that they have chosen a poor way to implement their strategy. The current rules, as stated in the Terms of Use, make no sense. In particular, according to Article 2, users must agree to absurd conditions, like — clause (i) — "not posting User Content that may create a risk of harm, loss, physical or mental injury, emotional distress, death, disability, disfigurement, or physical or mental illness to you, to any other person, or to any animal". Virtually any content I post will create *some* risk of causing emotional distress to *someone*, so it is impossible for me to comply with this rule. The Goodreads management are indeed within their rights if they want to remove content, but they have achieved that end by creating a situation in which virtually everyone is arguably breaking the rules. They have now exacerbated the situation by creating new rules defining content which will be deleted immediately and without warning. The new rules make even less sense than the old ones, and are not being applied systematically. This is surely not a good solution.

As several people have already pointed out, a more straightforward and honest way to write the ToU would be for Goodreads simply to say that they reserve the right, at their discretion, to remove any content, in particular content which they reasonably consider may cause physical, emotional or economic injury to another member of the site. In order to protect the expectation on the part of members that content will not be arbitrarily deleted, they would in addition pledge, except in extraordinary circumstances, not to remove content without giving users adequate warning and an explanation. This was until very recently the *de facto* policy, and it seemed to work well. It was not however part of the formal rules.

We have plenty of lawyers among our reviewers. I wonder if someone with the necessary skills could draft a couple of paragraphs intended to replace the current Article 2 with something along the basic lines of the above, so we could have a concrete alternative to discuss. My guess is that it wouldn't need to be very long or complicated. If it were done in a sensible and timely fashion, there might be a chance of reaching an amicable solution before people start leaving in earnest.

Or of course we could just continue as we are now. Destruction is also beautiful and satisfying in its way.

Part V

Revolt

Tired of apparently arbitrary deletions and a lack of meaningful answers from Goodreads management, the protesters began to take direct action in the hope of attracting some attention. Two suggestions were posted by Manny as reviews of Thoreau's *Civil Disobedience* and Evslin's *The Hydra*.

The second of these, in particular, became popular: when a review was deleted, other protesters aimed to replace it with several copies. The idea was soon tested when the original Hydra review was deleted as "off-topic". People first posted simple copies, which were deleted with the explanation that it was not permitted to post material that had already been posted by other members (a newly added rule). In response, the protesters started to post increasingly fanciful variants. Some of these were deleted and others allowed to stand, without any obvious pattern being apparent. Many protesters were notified that their accounts could be removed if they continued to post material of this kind. In several cases, they ignored the warnings without any accounts actually being closed down.

Arthur Graham found a new twist when he created an entry for the fictitious book *The Great Goodreads Censorship Debacle*, by G.R. McGoodreader; the creation of this kind of entry was an established type of humorous activity on the site, and many already existed. His idea was widely acclaimed, and members posted 78 reviews within a couple of days. No one was particularly surprised when Goodreads deleted the book from the database, but, as was quickly pointed out, they were breaking their own rules in doing so.

A Review of "Civil Disobedience"

Along with thousands of other people here, I am appalled by the recent changes on Goodreads. They prompted me to look at the Terms of Use, something I hadn't done for a long time. I was even more appalled to find that they are so restrictive that I am breaking them all the time. Look in particular at this passage from Article 2:

> You agree not to post User Content that: (i) may create a risk of harm, loss, physical or mental injury, emotional distress, death, disability, disfigurement, or physical or mental illness to you, to any other person, or to any animal; (ii) may create a risk of any other loss or damage to any person or property; (iii) seeks to harm or exploit children by exposing them to inappropriate content, asking for personally identifiable details or otherwise; (iv) may constitute or contribute to a crime or tort; (v) contains any information or content that we deem to be unlawful, harmful, abusive, racially or ethnically offensive, defamatory, infringing, invasive of personal privacy or publicity rights, harassing, humiliating to other people (publicly or otherwise), libelous, threatening, profane, or otherwise objectionable; (vi) contains any information or content that is illegal (including, without limitation, the disclosure of insider information under securities law or of another party's trade secrets); or (vii) contains any information or content that you do not have a right to make available under any law or under contractual or fiduciary relationships; or (viii) contains any information or content that you know is not correct and current.

The clauses I am most surprised by are (v) and (viii). I do not even see how it is possible to follow (v): how can I agree not to post content which "we" (who, exactly?) may deem "profane or otherwise objectionable", when these are entirely subjective criteria? I obviously don't know what some unnamed people in the Goodreads administration may deem objectionable. Clause (viii) is nearly as bad, and means that I am technically in default of the Terms of Use any time I post something that isn't a straight factual review.

Of course, Goodreads isn't deleting everything that contravenes these absurd rules. But the fact is that if they want to delete something I've written I'll be in a poor position to complain, given that I've clearly been breaking them. I dislike the fact that I've been turned into a criminal who is only allowed to carry on using the service because of the administrators' tolerance and forebearance.

Given that the rules are utterly stupid, it seems to me that the most constructive thing I can do is to follow them. Until they are changed, my policy will thus be to flag anyone who appears to be ignoring Article 2, in particular clauses (v) and (viii).[16] I have for example flagged Paul for his brilliant but non-factual review of *The Wind-Up Bird Chronicle*:[17]

> **Message 270** by Manny   Sep 23, 2013 02:14 am
>
> Flagged with following text:
>
> I am sorry, but I have to flag this review, which contravenes the Terms of Use. In particular, it fails to conform to Article 2 (viii), *You agree not to post User Content that ... contains any information or content that you know is not correct and current.*
>
> To take just one example, I find it very hard to believe

---

[16]I decided not long after that it was even more fun to flag reviews that were in default of clause (i); virtually any imaginable review creates some risk of causing emotional distress to someone. Trying to set a good example, I voluntarily retired my popular but rather negative review of the Harry Potter series. It was abundantly clear from the comment thread that it not only *could*, but indeed *had* caused emotional distress to several loyal Potter fans.

[17]https://www.goodreads.com/review/show/122557470

that Mr. Bryant has ever met "a random 16 year old girl who had a wooden leg and a parrot on her shoulder", who "suggested that [he] help her make some easy money by counting bald people." To be blunt, I believe he has fabricated this piquant detail.

You could perhaps send the reviewer a warning asking him to correct these evident inaccuracies, and delete the review if he fails to comply.

I have similarly flagged Ian for his creative but implausible review of *Mein Kampf*.[18]

> **Message 8** by Manny 22 hours, 10 minutes ago
>
> Flagged with following justification:
>
> I am flagging this review, which violates Article 2 of the Terms of Use: *You agree not to post User Content that ... contains any information or content that you know is not correct and current.* Ian is not currently serving a prison term at Bezoberg am Lech, and he is well aware of this. I suggest that you ask him to amend all factual inaccuracies, and delete it if he does not comply within a reasonable period.

And I have taken particular pleasure in flagging Mark's brief review of *An Uncommon Whore*,[19] which was not just factually incorrect but also highly insulting:

> **Message 1** by Manny Sep 23, 2013 02:23am
>
> Flagged with following justification:
>
> I would like to flag this review, which is factually inaccurate. Contrary to what the reviewer says, it is not

---

[18] https://www.goodreads.com/review/show/726502765
[19] Later deleted for being "off-topic".

about the acquisition of Goodreads by Amazon. It is, rather, about a guy who lets himself get fucked up the ass for money, and makes no reference to Goodreads whatsoever.

If you want to start playing this game and aren't sure who to flag, you're more than welcome to start with me. As already noted, I am a serial offender. For example, I freely admit that all of the following reviews contain "information or content that I knew was not correct and current":

- My review of *Fifty Shades of Grey*:[20] there is no such thing as the "Goodreads Center for Bodice-Ripping, Bondage and Twilight Studies".

- My review of *Quicksilver*:[21] I have not been visited by a time-traveler from the 25th century.

- My review of *The Martian Way*:[22] I have never constructed an anti-gravity machine from spare parts bought at a CERN garage sale and used it to fly to Jupiter.

- My review of *Emmanuelle*:[23] Bertrand Russell did not write a book called *Principia Sexualis* and try to sell the movie rights.

I'm just scraping the surface; there's plenty more.

Happy Flagging!

---

[20] https://www.goodreads.com/review/show/315359201
[21] https://www.goodreads.com/review/show/40092365
[22] https://www.goodreads.com/review/show/629249051
[23] https://www.goodreads.com/review/show/42382760

The Hydra

In the shower just now, I suddenly had a Eureka moment. The aspect of this current censorship war that's been upsetting us most is the feeling of powerlessless. Goodreads can arbitrarily change the rules, and they hardly even bother to respond when we complain. But we are not powerless. There are twenty million of us, and only a few dozen of them. We just need to get a little more organized, and we can easily resist.

So here's one concrete way to do it, based on the legend of Hercules. You will recall that Hercules had a difficult time against the Lernean Hydra; every time he cut off one of its heads, ten more grew back. We can do the same thing if we adopt the following plan:

1. Back up all your reviews, so that you have a copy of everything you have posted.

2. If you think that one of your reviews has been unreasonably deleted by Goodreads, repost it with an image of the Hydra at the top.

3. If you see someone else posting a Hydra review, make a copy of it and post it yourself.

We can improve this basic scheme with a little thought; for example, it would be better to have a place where we keep HTML marked-up source of reviews, so that they can immediately be reposted with the same formatting, and we need a plan for duplicating deleted shelves. But we can sort that out later. Without getting too bogged down in the details, I'm sure you see what will happen. The net result of Goodreads unreasonably deleting a review will be that it immediately comes back in many different places.

People who know their Greek mythology will be aware that Hercules did in fact defeat the Hydra, and Goodreads can use the same method if they dare; they can close down the account of anyone who participates in the scheme. That will work, but I am not sure that anything less drastic will be effective. I think Goodreads will be reluctant to escalate to this level. A large proportion of the most active reviewers are now part of the protest movement, and they would be losing much of the content that makes the site valuable. Even more to the point, the media have already started to get interested (maybe you saw the article in the Washington Post). They would love the story, and it would create a mountain of bad publicity for Goodreads and Amazon.

I'd say the odds are heavily in our favor. Why don't we try it? I promise now to respond to any Hydra calls.

A Hysteria of Hydras

(licensed by Wolfgang Sauber under CC-BY-SA 3.0: `http://commons.wikimedia.org/wiki/File:`
`Lernaean\_Hydra\_Getty\_Villa\_83.AE.346.jpg)`

Greek vase hydra

(licensed by Classical Numismatic Group, Inc. `http://www.cngcoins.com` *under CC-BY-SA 3.0:*
`http://commons.wikimedia.org/wiki/File:Ercole\_Hydra\_76001812.jpg)`

Numismatic hydra

(licensed by Kerotan under CC-BY 3.0 based on a photo by Luis García licensed under CC-BY-SA 2.0 Generic:

http://commons.wikimedia.org/wiki/File:Sockpuppet-hydra.jpeg)

Mosaic hydra

(Creative Commons Attribution 3.0 Unported license:
http://glendonmellow.blogspot.de/2011/03/sock-puppet-hydra11.html)

Sock puppet hydra

(Public domain: http://commons.wikimedia.org/wiki/File:Hydra_04.jpg)

Renaissance German hydra

A ToU-Compliant Hydra

My original review of *The Hydra* was removed by Goodreads yesterday for being "potentially off-topic." I have posted it under "My Writings", where hopefully it does not violate any guidelines.

Below I have written a different review about *The Hydra* which should be fully compliant with the clearly delineated Goodreads Book Report Guidelines to Ensure Topical Reviews (GRBRGETR) v. 1.0001 (revised 9-20-2013).

This book report is about the book *The Hydra*. The Hydra was a monster in ancient Greece that had a lot of heads. If you cut a head off it grew more heads. The heads were bad because they were so poisonous even their breath could kill you. Just when you thought you killed it two more heads came back so it was very hard to kill and dangerous.

Hercules was a very strong hero. Hera told him he had to kill the Hydra. But she knew he would most likely get killed because of all the heads. He tried with arrows and swords and clubs but he couldn't kill it. He had to hold his breath because of the poisonous Hydra breath. The more heads he crushed the more came back.

[spoiler: Hercules got some help from a friend to burn up the heads so Hercules could cut off the immortal head and stick it under a rock. That was sort of cheating. But in those days they did not have Scope.]

The story of the Hydra is a good story. Also it can be a metaphor for trying to beat something that just keeps growing back stronger. And also with more heads. A metaphor is something that can represent something else.

Like an example from real life that the Hydra reminds me of is when people try to make other people not say bad stuff on the Internet.

That is hard to do because you can stop them in one place but then the bad ideas pop up somewhere else even worse than before and with even worse breath. It's like the game Whack-a-Mole which is kind of a dumb game.

(licensed by Malcolm Koo under CC-BY-SA 2.0 Generic:
`http://commons.wikimedia.org/wiki/File\%3AWhac-A-Mole\_machine.jpg)`

This was a good book because it made me think a lot about Hydras. Also it made me think about some other things too even though I tried not to. Sometimes I have that problem with books. But I did not talk about those other things in my book report.

An Excited YA Hydra

I am still unsure about the accepted methods of writing book-reports reviewing on Goodreads. But I seem to think the following is not in violation of the GR review-writing policies.

WHEEEEEEEEEEEEEEEEEEEEEEEEEEEEEEEEEEE!

ZOMG! OMFG! $&%$#%@&*$^#(%@%&&^%

I'm so excited for the hydra err this book. The excitement is not for the book's release or anything since it released like decades ago.

I am excited for the sake of being excited. And also because it is okay to post these animated-gif-filled, braincell-destroying non-reviews if they are positive, do not mention anything remotely related to bad author behavior and if they are understandably in the self-published YA/NA/Erotica section. Since the esteemed GR management only deletes 'potentially off-topic' reviews which go against or do not serve their business interests.

Okay continuing with my excitement for this book ... ...

hyperventilates

That hydra on the cover looks so

sexxxxxxxxxxyyyyyyyyyyyyyyyyyyyyyyyyyyyyy.

I am really, truly excited about this book although I have very little idea about what it is. So I heard there's Hercules in it and a hydra whose heads he lops off one after another but for every head he cuts off, 10 more of them grow back.

Ugh talk about **gross!** But heck I like it because it eerily seems like an allegory of a virtual world scenario to me. I am sure it is reminiscent of something happening on a site whose name starts with a "G" and ends with an "S". I can't remember what this something or this site is though.

I can't wait to conveniently order the costliest version of this available on Amazon and make Jeff Bezos richer by a few dollars and then hopefully proceed to write a review like —

"Ooooh I absolutely, truly, surely, certainly, undoubtedly loved

loveeeeeeeeeeeeed

this book. I loved all the characters ... and the hydra. 5++++++++++ stars" just so it motivates other book buyers to contribute towards making Bezos a gazillionaire sooner rather than later.

WHEEEEEEEEEEEEEEEEEEEEEEEEEEEEEEEE!

Really really really looking forward to the hydra.

PS — Are you wondering what happened to the gifs in the review? In the war between dignity and being ironic, dignity won.

An Electronic Quotational Hydra

This allegorical novel is about a half-Manny/half-water monster who like Archimedes had a Eureka moment while water was streaming down his reptilian back. This Postmodernist novel is a metaphor for the effect of a Herculean reader's site that imposes arbitrary censorship on its reviewers. The apparent deconstruction by this Hercules on the Hydra's head only sprouted more heads. This meta-meta of a reality within a reality is best demonstrated by the review within a review. This is my very own picture taken with my very own iPad of Manny's review, with his approval.

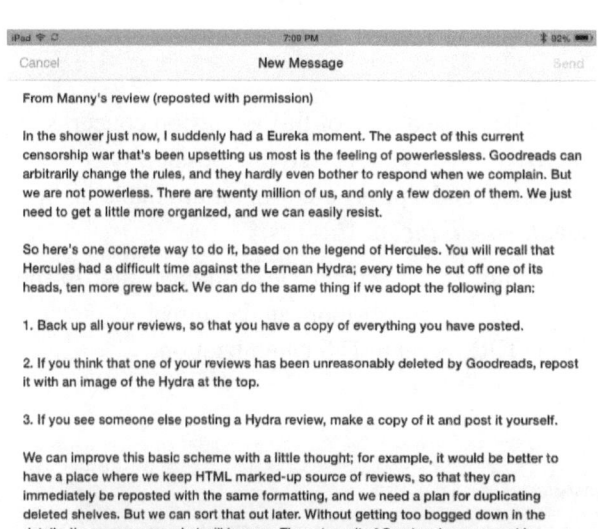

A Derridean Hydra

A second edition of this Hydra review has been commission'd. Publication is not yet scheduled. We are just in the beginning stages of this project, taking into account everything which we will have learned already (always) about the mythological beast known as The Hydra from Bernard Evslin's retelling of this ancient tale; a tale which seems to resonate with us down through the ages even unto the cyber-21st century. Meanwhile, here's what we have for you today as a Look-Inside feature:

To quote : "The second case of this exclusion concerns our subject more directly. It involves precisely the possibility for every performative utterance (and a priori every other utterance) to be 'quoted.'" — Derrida, *Limited, Inc*, p. 16.

And so the following is written, ie, "quoted", not in the spirit of erasure *a priori*, but much more under threat of erasure; a threat arising from OUR threat to ITS capitalization.

[begin spoiler]

...

Well, anyways...

This stuff about quotations is sooo 1970's. Today, we just need a hyperlink; the hyghway to hyper-literarinesseseses.

`https://www.goodreads.com/story/show/349203-off-topic?chapter=3`

But even hyperlinkers need to eat. Here's the meat:

> 1. Back up all your reviews, so that you have a copy of everything you have posted.

2. If you think that one of your reviews has been unreasonably deleted by Goodreads, repost it with an image of the Hydra at the top.

3. If you see someone else posting a Hydra review, make a copy of it and post it yourself.

— Fist-Fucking-Pump!

As an add-on, but not an integral part of this project to preserve your thoughts, your thoughts PUBLICly expressed, and in fact, quite distinct from this Hydrical-Archival project, you may solicit FLAGS. That's just an option. Don't be an unethical asshole and Flag stuff when no Flagging has been solicited. [myself? I don't solicit. thank you]

...

[end spoiler]

And to close the bracket, ~~demonstrating that under Fair Use conventions, I have, despite the extended deployment of the quotation punctuation, recontextualized the above freely distributed content, a right always retained by the rights=holder and freely given, and~~ I offer you a second quotation, "Standing in the Shower Thinking":

http://www.youtube.com/watch?v=Q_3oOUfpdVY

An Angry Hydra

Fellow Goodreader Manny wrote a review for this book that has since been deleted. He felt that users of this community could do something about the censorship blather regarding the terms of service here on Goodreads using the Hydra Principle. After enacting my part of this little protest, I received an email that my review of this book (and others) were removed due to non-original content. I also had been issued a warning that I'd be removed from the site if I persisted.

After some reflection, I realized they are right. I really should put my own original content in my review. This lead me to think that we've misapplied this myth to our present reality.

You see, the Hydra creature reminds me less of Goodreads users and more of Goodreads themselves. Cut the head off the Hydra and it would grow back, twofold. Such with GoodReads; with each question unanswered, each review deleted, and each instance of content censored, they grow **more** and **more** noxious.

Ever the naïve dreamer, I imagined that there were human beings on the other side of this mess capable of independent thought and communication. I failed, utterly, to understand that I cannot apply humanistic thoughts or feelings to the Hydra. The Hydra is a thing, an animal, a gross creation. The Hydra's whole purpose was to cause hopelessness and despair in the hero (or, alternately, to sell more books).

I disappoint myself really. It's too bad that Goodreads management, interns, admin, employees, whoever the f*ck they are that are making these red button decisions, have the ability to separate their own souls from the corporate machine. It's sad that not one single being in those powers that be can act with some integrity. I guess innovation in customer service within social media sphere is a pipe dream. After all, most of this entire slugfest is because of **lack of communication**. How absurd.

Goodreads is the monster here, not the users. You can apply that how you will. They could easily be portrayed in Hydra-like hideousness, or Godzilla-like enormity. For me, I'm starting to think of them as the proverbial monster under the bed, harmless unless I let my imagination run away with me. Goodreads means as much to me as I do to them.

I always understood that having my account deleted was a possibility, but didn't have a lot to lose because without a vibrant community to participate (read: lurk) in, Goodreads is nothing but a cataloging tool.

G.R. McGoodreader: An Eyewitness Account

The book entry for *The Great Goodreads Censorship Debacle* was created on Saturday, October 12, 2013 by Arthur Graham. Although the description was brief, it struck a chord and was soon the object of intense study:

> A story of Goodreads. A story of betrayal. A story unlike any other reviewed before on this website. Is it a dystopian novel? Is it a nonfiction treatise on GR policy? Or is it an incarnation of this debacle itself? Like all books, this may be for you, the reader, to decide.

The mystery was only deepened by the tantalizingly incomplete biography on the home page of its hitherto unknown author, G.R. McGoodreader:

> G.R. McGoodreader was born on a Friday afternoon, when his parents thought nobody would notice.
>
> Life at home in his early days was turbulent, but he was mostly ignored and his cries fell on deaf ears.
>
> As he grew up, he engaged in a number of forms of civil disobedience, with varying degrees of (i.e. no) success.
>
> G.R.'s books include *The Great Goodreads Censorship Debacle* (forthcoming) and *Yes, I Farted* (2013), which is shortlisted for the American Natural Gas Alliance Literary Prize.
>
> Forthcoming from the Goodreads community.

People soon found that McGoodreader's author page had also been created by Graham. A dozen theories sprang up. The most common one, held by some 99.8% of the Goodreads membership, was admittedly that the book did not exist and had been concocted by the inventive Mr. Graham, based on a suggestion from fellow-protester Clouds. But several productive GR reviewers, who through no fault of their own were currently resident at the Magnitogorsk Institute for the Congenitally Insane, stalwartly maintained, in broken English larded with Russianisms, that it was genuine. In the absence of clear proof one way or the other, one had to admit that the truth of the matter was unknown.

The tantalizing uncertainty concerning the author and the topical nature of the book combined to create lively interest in the Goodreads community, and many people (I was one) posted speculative reviews. My own effort, which if I remember correctly received over 70 votes, read as follows:

> My favorite bit was the graphic dream sequence where the naive and grasping Sito is anally raped by the evil Nozama. I am not sure I understand the symbolism; some reviewers argue that the Japanese-sounding names signal an allusion to Mishima, but I cannot help feeling that another interpretation is possible. I am almost sure that some vital clue is staring me in the face.

You may wonder how I knew about this passage; it is possible that I will reveal further details in due course.

Despite his instant fame, Mr. McGoodreader did not appear to have a sanguine view of his future prospects. People noted that the only "forthcoming event" listed on the book's home page was a curt note that it would be deleted the following day, and this prediction did indeed come to pass. Book and author alike were universally mourned throughout the Goodreads community.

During its brief existence, *The Great Goodreads Censorship Debacle* had collected an impressive total of 95 ratings and 78 reviews. By way of comparison, Russell and Whitehead's magisterial *Principia Mathematica*, arguably the most important book ever written on formal logic, has in over four years accumulated only 158 ratings and a miserable 4 reviews, one of which consists entirely of repetitions of the word "rhubarb". It is impossible not to wonder what McGoodeader could have achieved had he lived longer. Comparisons with John F. Kennedy, though arguably *mal à propos*, were inevitable.

Did McGoodreader and his book really exist? Who deleted their pages? No one, except possibly the inmates of the Magnitogorsk Institute, knows the answers to these questions. The affair has become the great unsolved mystery of Goodreads. Some of the newer members have even begun to say that there never was a G.R. McGoodreader. We old-timers, who were around during those fateful early October days, smile when we hear them. I know. I was there. I saw the screens with my own eyes. For once, I was privileged to witness a moment of history, and that memory will live with me all my life.

McGoodreader came, he posted, and he departed; we shall not look on his like again.

Wanted

(licensed by Nandakishore under CC-BY-ND 3.0)

Part VI

The aftermath

The popularity of the Hydra protest seemed to have the effect of discouraging Goodreads management from continuing to delete their posts. Instead, they went back to removing reviews commenting on author behavior, again choosing the ones to be deleted on apparently arbitrary grounds.

The general chaos on the site made it an increasingly unattractive place to be, and the rival site BookLikes reported record numbers of new members. Manny posted detailed instructions for moving content to BookLikes in the shape of a review of *Moving for Dummies*. This was also deleted as "off-topic". When reposted in a different area, it was however ignored. There appeared to be an uneasy stalemate between the two opposing forces.

Many people posted complaints about the toxic atmosphere, most often blaming it on Goodreads management and Amazon, but sometimes on the protesters.

A Review of "Gazelle"

Please do not DELETE this Review.

Please do not FLAG this Review.

My reviews are on strike. The arbitrary deletion policy which Goodreads management has been practicing must stop. At the very least, they must negotiate with us in good faith.

I have thrown in with the monkey-wrenchers and sabot-tossers.

I do believe that there exist Reviews which ought to be deleted. But only *I* have the authority to do so; however, I do not (fortunately) have the power.

As a laborer and (minor) producer of content and value for the entity 'Goodreads' I reserve the right to withhold my labor. I will no longer write reviews; until the threat of arbitrary deletion is lifted. I may continue to write Reviews like this one which will have nothing to do with the book. Nothing.

Please do not FLAG my Reviews. I am Amish enough to not willingly submit to the violence of secular authority. There is no need to bring anything I write to the attention of Goodreads management. I do not, and never have, written for their benefit.

Please do not FLAG my Reviews. I do not want management to be consistent about deleting reviews. I want them to stop deleting ANY reviews.

I will also cease using the silly star-system. The star-system has, from the beginning of both Amazon and Goodreads, always been designed to commodify books.

I do not believe that there has ever been a Golden Age of Goodreads when we were all just an innocuous little book club. From the beginning, Goodreads was designed to aggregate capital, to become a desirable object for purchase/take-over. The policies which management began to implement in September would also have been eventually implemented even without Amazon's interest in *Gleichschaltung*.

I am not going anywhere. This is *my* fucking territory. I am not Amish enough to emigrate when my way of life is threatened.

post scriptum: with sincerest apologies to all my Friends, each one Dear, who would like to continue using Goodreads as we have been accustomed to do.

A Review of "Moving for Dummies"

If you're wondering who the dummy is in the title of this book, it's me. I was such a dummy that I thought it would be difficult and time-consuming to move my content from Goodreads to BookLikes. But when Goodreads deleted three of my reviews the other day and sent me a mail threatening to close down my account, I decided I'd better look into the details. I discover that it is in fact extremely simple. Here's what I did:

1. I went to the Goodreads import/export page and clicked on "export to a csv file" (top right).

2. This produced a CSV file, which I saved in a sensible place.

3. I opened a BookLikes account.

4. I went to the BookLikes import page and clicked on "Import books from Goodreads: Choose file", giving the name of the CSV file where I'd saved my exported data in (2).

5. I clicked on "Import books from Goodreads: Import".

Then I just sat back and let it do the importing until it sent me a mail to say it was finished. I looked at a few sample reviews and shelves, and everything I checked seemed fine. My total investment of time was a few minutes.

It's improved my peace of mind considerably. Try it yourself.

A note to the manager of the Goodreads employee responsible for the new censorship policy

As a direct result of your subordinate's actions, one of your most loyal reviewers has just copied all his Goodreads content to a site that is directly competing with you. He has also posted detailed instructions showing three thousand friends and followers how to do the same thing.

You may wish to spend a moment thinking about whether this person is an asset or a liability to your company.

The Art of War: Corporate Takeover of User Rights

"If you don't pay for the product, then you're not the customer, you're the product", media analysts told us plainly a long time ago.

Be that as it may, the Goodreads experience has both common and unique features. The past years have seen MySpace rise and fall, Facebook shamelessly mocking users' privacy and still going on, Twitter changing their API according to the phase of the moon and keeping personal data hidden from users, Google purging G+ of "fake names" (that's pen names for us, booknerds!) and so on and so on.

These corporations have taken over the Internet. You, the user, receive a service for free, to relate with your friends, to keep your personal photos, to share your thoughts on the books you've read. You're targeted by advertising, your personal data is being stored on the company's servers, and, sooner than you think, you're dependent on these companies because of social networking, because you made yourself at home in a sub-community with your friends and preferred groups or reviewers. While you can get away (easier or harder), you leave behind content, topics, friends and functionality you got used to.

Your Content and Social Interaction Belong to Them

These corporate services keep control over users in three ways:

1. Proprietary service

The software is on the company's servers, and nowhere else. It's not available to users, no one knows how it works and what or how data is processed for storage, for reading (private data), for security and logging, for auditing, for removals.

2. Overreaching ToS

Under the excuse of needing it to function or to defend their business, the company takes more rights for itself over user content than actually necessary. The Goodreads Terms of Use are particularly misleading because the company claims all sub-rights of copyright, while telling users that they keep copyright (it's true, but they took all rights to do anything with the content, *anything at all*). The ToU are also contradictory and impossible to abide by. Really. Since users usually don't read the fine print, they assume common sense. Which is not that common after all.

3. Reduced inter-operatibility for data exchange

These sites are silos of content under a company's control. There are more or less features to retrieve your data, and more or less APIs to build alternative clients. On the first, GR stands well, compared to others. You can send your review to a blog on two sites when you post it, you can export a CVS file with your reviews. (Only reviews, no topics, no comments, but other sites have nothing). On the second, the API seems relatively poor, compared to what it could provide.

The Art of War against user rights: proprietary service, misleading on copyright, lack of inter-operability with other sites or applications.

Aside from common traits shared by any proprietary service, there are essential differences, here on Goodreads.

Community librarians

Goodreads's mission has been to create a public database of all books ever published. GR has provided the software online, but it is community *librarians* who have added to and maintained this database, providing their work for free, tens of thousands of record edits, over the years. The GR site has acquired its market value through the work of its community.

And it's this work they sold out to Amazon earlier this year.

A site for readers

Goodreads has been known and advertised as "a site for readers", to interact and share their opinions in book reviews and group conversations. The site has thousands of well-written, intellectually pleasing reviews, free essays prompted by the book, and opinionated pieces by booklovers all over the world.

Nowadays, the success or failure of a book in the digitized and self-published world is no longer in the traditional, professional outlets alone, it's in the popularity and free dissemination of information by readers who shared their thoughts on this site.

The value of this site has always been MORE the work of the users, than other services enumerated above. The GR community is not randomly composed of users signing up only for personal interest and personal friends (or marketing), as in other social networks. It has been created by people working together on the book library, by their reviews, by their blogs.

TODAY ...

Some of these reviews are now removed. Some bookshelves that refer to author behavior are now removed (and others remain). Reviews that inform readers that a children's book author was convicted of pedophilia (!) have been removed from the site. Reviews that use the book for an essay on GR/Amazon or on the good faith shown by startups, or on illogical terms in corporate ToUs, have been removed. Reviews re-posting content of the removed reviews have been removed in their turn.

Some of top 25 reviewers on this site are threatened by GR/Amazon with removal of their account. Paul Bryant's reviews, Manny's reviews, have been deemed "potentially off-topic" and have been deleted.

...I can see how the issue of exercising corporate control over users content is truly enraging here, on a site significantly made by these contributors. It's unavoidable that we come to this, in my opinion (corporations always do), and GR/Amazon has all the keys to the kingdom, but I can see why it's so disappointing and enraging. Your content is theirs to do with as they please, their software works as they want, your choices are take it or leave it.

The Internet is no longer for sharing (nor for porn!), it's for corporations to exercise their control over users.

Community Power

Goodreaders have started protests all over the place. Many reviews have been posted, in protest, arguing their points against GR/Amazon actions. Many of them have been removed.

Irony and sarcasm abound, in reviews posted the last week, in topics in Goodreads Feedback group, and on remote sites. Many of the reviews have been removed, some of the topics have been closed. Rounds of ironic flagging have been made; flags claiming to abide by the ToS language in its inept and auto-contradictory "rules" have been sent to GR staff, in the hope they'll come to their senses. They seem to have missed the irony.

The only long-term solution to corporate control is to create competitive services based on the principles of freedom of users. In all three aspects: Open Source software, same license for content for the service as for other users (or minimal for it to function), and inter-operability of networked services.

Part VII

Goodbye letters

It became more and more common to see posts from people announcing their intention to leave the site. Some of these were humorous, but most were deeply distressed.

The general feeling was that the breakdown in relations between members and management was a tragedy, irrespective of who was to blame.

The Goodreads Censorship Rap

I have a story to tell, so listen up well
It's the reason why reviewers decided to rebel
It'll make you angry, you might just spit
But I'll tell you all how this awesome book site went straight to shit

I'm a bibliophile by nature and I really dislike clichés
But reviewing books on Goodreads is what I did with most of my days
Hanging out with super nerds who were actually pretty cool
Readin' tons of books even though I've been done graduated from school
But then a couple of authors didn't get the site fully
Started making trouble and calling out ... wait for it ... "BULLY!"
I got in a few Internet brawls and Goodreads got scared
They said "We're deletin' a few of your reviews, neener neener, so there!"

I was angry and frustrated day after day
That a site that I'd championed for could treat me this way
They didn't budge, they were serious, but the part that really blew?
Them telling me to keep acting like this and "your account will come under review"

So to BookLikes I ventured and it wasn't half bad
They were happy to welcome refugees and even held our hands
Maybe this is what real customer care is like?
I suppose we could all get used to that, amirite?

Too many of my friends are leaving right and left
They're outraged at this full-out content theft
I see their protests, I hear their cries
They're screaming this place's no longer legit
Congrats, Goodreads! I hope all that Amazon money was worth it.

My 3100 Words on the Evils Of Censorship and the Wrongness of Breaking Trust

Goodreads, I hardly knew ye.

I joined in 2010, and I became an active member in 2011. Less than two years later, I'm beginning the process of ratcheting my activity down to virtually zero. In those two years, I had a blast and a wonderful streak of lucky friendships and some great reviewing fortune. I've amassed a following of about 1600 people, become a "Forbes 25 Top Reviewers" member, been in the top-ten most popular reviewers measured, by Goodreads, every week or month for most of 2012 and 2013. That's a wonderful, wonderful experience for anyone to have.

Then Amazon bought Goodreads, and my "uh-oh" light went on. Otis Chandler, founder of Goodreads, announced this in April 2013. The Feedback forum on the site went bonkers. That forum consists of about 13,000 people, out of a reported 20 million members. A tiny, tiny minority ... but a vocal and passionate minority committed to working on a site that allowed its members to, for free, catalog and discuss their books with a vibrant and opinionated community of likewise vocal and passionate readers of books. The price? Look at the ads. (And not even that if you, like me, have AdBlocker on your browser.) Goodreads asked us if we minded them sharing our popular reviews with third parties, as an extra revenue-generating measure. I myownself agreed readily. I wanted to help the site survive, to maintain its independence.

The announcement of the sale chilled me to the bone. All the posts I made about the sale are gone, deleted with the thread that contained them, in May 2013. Otis Chandler decided to distill the conversation into a series of FAQs.[24] I'm reproducing a few select questions with some responses bolded for emphasis:

---

[24] https://www.goodreads.com/topic/show/1337250-faqs-on-amazon-s-acquisition-of-goodreads

Editing of reviews — can Goodreads or Amazon edit my reviews? Delete them without asking?

Nothing has changed when it comes to reviews. Your reviews are yours and we value the frank and honest opinions of all our members. That's what makes Goodreads different and special. (And yes, you can continue to swear if that's important to you, include images, etc.)

Our policy has been and will continue to be that we never edit a member's review. In some cases — where the review has broken our guidelines — we will delete the review, just as we have in the past.

There is one situation — and again this has been our policy for a long time — where we might use part of your review without showing the whole review. Sometimes, an author or publisher will ask to use a snippet of a book review in an advertisement outside of Goodreads or on a book's back cover. Rather than include the full review, they will use a line or two. This is similar to what you see in ads for movies. We always check with the members who wrote the reviews before granting permission. If an author or a publisher wants to use an excerpt of a book review in an ad on Goodreads, our team will review the ad and we permit this without checking with the reviewer as members are already sharing this content on Goodreads. These are policies that we already had in place and they have not changed.

Will sales targets or sponsorships now influence how reviews appear on the book page and which book recommendations I see on the site?

From the very beginning of Goodreads, we have always had a very firm policy about ensuring that editorial content on the site is never influenced by advertising. This isn't changing.

We'll also continue to show reviews in the same order as before:

- Reviews by your friends (people you know and trust)
- Reviews by people whose reviews you have chosen to follow (people whose opinion and taste in books you trust)
- Reviews from the Goodreads community, sorted by our proprietary algorithm.

As for recommendations, our proprietary algorithms analyze 20 billion data points to come up with personalized book recommendations. Advertising is not part of this process and won't be in the future.

Will Goodreads now be more focused on being a site for authors?

We love having authors on Goodreads. But, we are a site that's focused on readers first. If there is a choice between what is best for readers and what is best for authors, we will always err on the side of readers. It's right there in how we describe ourselves: "the largest site for readers and book recommendations."

On the other hand, lots of readers love to have direct interaction with their favorite authors and we're happy to provide a platform for that to happen.

For new authors looking to establish themselves and build awareness of their books, **we'll continue to educate them on the best way to interact on Goodreads. It's a learning process and our key advice will always be: first and foremost, be a reader on Goodreads.**

All that sounds very reassuring. No plans to change, no one will notice a difference. Then came Banned Books Week and, ironically on the Friday before the celebration of resisting censorship began, an announcement that Goodreads is deleting the reviews and, later on, the shelves labeled in a manner that focuses attention on the author of a book and not the book itself. Kara, the Director of Customer Care, posted this in response to massive numbers of protest posts on the "Important Note Regarding Reviews" thread where the surprise was revealed:

> We've been reading all the comments and wanted to give an update based on some of the concerns in the thread.
>
> To clarify, we haven't deleted any book reviews in regard to this issue. [Not strictly speaking true. See below.] The key word here is "book". The reviews that have been deleted — and that we don't think have a place on Goodreads — are reviews like "the author is an a**hole and you shouldn't read this book because of that". In other words, they are reviews of the author's behavior and not relevant to the book. We believe books should stand on their own merit, and it seems to us that's the best thing for readers.
>
> Someone used the word censorship to describe this. **This is not censorship — this is setting an appropriate tone for a community site. We encourage members to review and shelve books in a way that makes sense for them, but reviews and shelves that focus primarily on author behavior do not belong on Goodreads.**

From Wikipedia, this definition of censorship:

> Censorship is the suppression of speech or other public communication which may be considered objection-

able, harmful, sensitive, politically incorrect or inconvenient as determined by a government, media outlet or other controlling body. It can be done by governments and private organizations or by individuals who engage in self-censorship. It occurs in a variety of different contexts including speech, books, music, films, and other arts, the press, radio, television, and the Internet for a variety of reasons including national security, to control obscenity, child pornography, and hate speech, to protect children, to promote or restrict political or religious views, and to prevent slander and libel. It may or may not be legal. Many countries provide strong protections against censorship by law, but none of these protections are absolute and it is frequently necessary to balance conflicting rights in order to determine what can and cannot be censored.

So yes indeed, the act of deleting reviews and other user-created materials suddenly deemed not-community-friendly is censorship. "Enforcing community standards" ... well ... just a question from the peanut gallery here, but how did this community standard get set, by whom, and when? A long and separate chat could be had on that topic. But for now. let's note there were 21 people whose reviews were, summarily and without warning, deleted. That contradicts what Kara said above. And she posted this update to backtrack from her earlier assertion:

> Thank you for all the comments so far. One concern that has come up in this thread is that the content was deleted without those members first being told that our moderation policy had been revised.
>
> In retrospect, we absolutely should have given users notice that our policies were changing before taking action on the items that were flagged. To the 21 members who were impacted: we'd like to sincerely apologize

> for jumping the gun on this. It was a mistake on our part, and it should not have happened.
>
> Anyone else with reviews or shelves created prior to September 21, 2013 that will be deleted under the revised policy will be sent a notification first and given time to decide what to do.
>
> Again, thank you for all your comments. We'll continue to monitor this thread for your feedback.

So we're all hunky-dory again, right? Warning will be given to people who fall afoul of the new "community standards" which we're now enforcing. Time to make a decision about revising content, moving content, what one wishes to do in response to the site's desire to remove one's content from its community's gaze. I wasn't given a warning, I was informed my content was removed:

> Hello Richard,
>
> Your review of The Hydra were [sic] recently brought to our attention. Please note that any reviews you post must contain your own original content (see our review guidelines). Any reviews that are simply copy-pasted duplicates of other reviews will be removed. Given this, the review in question has been deleted. We have attached a copy for your personal records.
>
> Additionally, your review of Civil Disobedience and Other Essays was recently flagged by Goodreads members as potentially off-topic. As the review is not about the book, it has been removed from the site. You can find the text of the review attached for your personal records.
>
> Please note that if you continue to violate our guidelines, your account may come under review for removal.
>
> Sincerely, The Goodreads Team

Now, I've been completely and publicly pantiwadulous over the major change in Terms of Use as they affect what reviewers ... the unpaid volunteers who create the value that Amazon paid for the company to get! ... can and cannot say to/about authors in their own reviews, and even more troublingly, what the reviewers can and cannot name the shelves or collections they put their books into. It didn't need to be personal to me to draw my attention to the many and various attempts to censor what kind of reading material is available to you, me, our kids, our grandkids, and the banning parties hope, posterity. Books that talk about S-E-X or the right of women to walk down all the streets of the world without fearing rape or the existence of this little thing called "science" that rejects religion's once-upon-a-time version of Creation get banned regularly ... until now, Goodreads has been a place to discuss these banned books freely and openly. How long before the author-friendly censorship moves into family-friendly censorship, such as the amorphous "community standards" Kara cites above will come to demand?

In the long run, censorship doesn't work. In the short run, it's hideously costly in human emotional terms, titanically wasteful of time, effort, and resources to police and enforce, and morally repugnant to right-thinking people.

But the evil doesn't stop at formal banning of a book, governmental or business anathema pronounced upon a writer, a press, a review ... those things, while reprehensible, are formal, out there for the public to see and hear and (theoretically) obey.

More insidious is a behavior that's meant to fly under the radar, such as deleting people's work without warning, but this is almost inevitable when these "community standards" that were never hashed out, publicly debated, or even made a topic of conversation are put in place by fiat. And when the actions are discovered, they're covered up by (factually correct, morally wrong) justifications like "Oh look how few people are actually affected!" and "Most of you will never know it's even there!" and "It's my concrete noun and I'll do as I goddamned well please with it."

To quote a religious figure of great renown, "Truly I tell you, whatever you did not do for one of the least of these, you did not do for me." (Matthew 31:45) You didn't speak up for the safety or the happiness of those piddling few? You didn't worry because it wasn't you?

Next time it will be. Or the time after that. Or the one after that. Because if I've learned nothing else in 54 years of relatively constant annoyance by earthlings, I've learned that the forces of Command and Control NEVER EVER STOP WANTING MORE.

I don't know if anyone on the Goodreads staff expected the strength and passion of delivery of the vitriol that the sheeple (irony there!) of the site unleashed on this decision. If they did not, they were not paying attention to the titanic kerfuffle when Amazon bought Goodreads. **Twenty-five hundred posts** (mostly) of outrage and fear didn't make an impact? The Ugly Green Button contretemps, with 2,350 posts, made a dent? Now there are over 5,800 posts on the Announcement thread linked above!

Goodreads folk are passionate and committed readers and writers. And the reason they've ... we've ... invested so much emotional energy in the site is, at base, simple. It's the only one of its kind, the only place where readers connect with other readers by means of reviews, groups, and serendipity. Competitors to Goodreads are a great deal smaller, they're often focused around special interests (e.g., LibraryThing, that unparalleled book cataloging site, with a sideline of social activity that's not very much encouraged), or they just haven't got the chops to make the ease and fluidity of opinion discovery on a par with Goodreads.

So naturally change will be resisted and feared by many, and just as naturally the Powers That Be will seek to direct the community's attention to such areas as will benefit the advertisers and/or owners who pay the bills. Some tension is inevitable, some compromise desirable on all sides. But to date, no compromise has been offered on any issue of site governance I've cited here. The policy announced Friday, 23 September 2013, that announces Goodreads can and will delete user-created information at will and without warning is in place. The mea-culpa issued the next week, with a reassurance that they won't delete stuff without warning again isn't, it appears, part of the formal policy yet.

This is put in place, we're told, because Goodreads wants to maintain a TONE, an atmosphere, of respect and tolerance. Because nothing says respect and tolerance like unilaterally changing a community-wide policy with a dump-and-run message on Friday afternoon, in a group that much less than 1% of the user base belongs to, right?

Still, it's their (well, Amazon's) site and they set the rules, right? Right. They do. And they offer the service to us for free, right, so they pretty much deserve to have a completely free hand, right?

Nope. Not without a fight.

I'm appalled by the dismissive snort many Goodreaders emit, essentially saying, "suck it up Buttercup, if you're not the paying customer you're the paid-for commodity." Point taken ... you don't value the existence of a cyberspace dedicated to free discussion of the ideas and impact of books on readers. Fine, then you're not required to be upset about the absence of such a cyberspace. But you still lose when ANY voice is silenced, out of fear or obedience or ... worst of all ... despair. How many honest reviews, negative to the author's feelings and even insulting in language, will now not be written? How many conversations will go un-had? (I've learned a lot from arguing my point's validity on my most vitriolic reviews.)

Talking about books freely and without censorship, whether internal or external in origin, is as important an activity as reading the damn things. If no one talks about *Mein Kampf*, or *Man and Superman*, or *The Hydra*, why kill the trees to print them? Why dedicate the bandwidth to delivering the files to the ereader screens? If people care enough to read even one book a year, shouldn't they be encouraged and supported in a desire to discuss it in full, even (or espeecially) if they aren't experts in literary theory or history or ethics or copyright?

Stifling one, twenty-one, a million and one, people's willingness to speak honestly and from the heart about the ideas, the words, the feelings expressed in a book, by an author, is stealing from the rest of us who are unaffected the very necessary challenge of understanding, if never accepting, a different point of view.

And that's what Goodreads was. Was. I have to use the past tense. It WAS this. It is now a data farm and sales platform for a bookselling entity. (Whose customer I am, by the way, and will continue to be, because I exist on less money per month that most of you make in a week.) And sales are hurt, the conventional wisdom goes, by shouting.

Goodreads was a unique thing, a place where opinions about books created by writers could be examined and opined upon without fear of censorship. That is an important function. No one else was doing it. And now, in fact, no one is doing it.

And that's the most horrible thing about censorship: To avoid falling afoul of the censors, we question ourselves and censor ourselves and make a big deal out of things in our heads. We do the work of the control freaks for them, out of a desire to avoid them.

Like Amazon, Goodreads reviews will steadily become less and less useful because, basically, how will I ever trust that the happy-clappy Kool-Aid dispensing Nicey McNiceToMe people haven't got hold of it?

Ray Bradbury said it best: "You don't have to burn books to destroy a culture. Just get people to stop reading them." And talking about them. And now there's no safe place to do that with the size audience, with their wallets ready to spring open.

The decline, it would seem, has accelerated, and the fall is imminent. I'm sad about that. For me, I'm going to shout from the wilderness. I'll post protests and I'll post reviews that are explicitly anti-censorship and tie them into these concerns. And most people will learn to ignore me, more than they already do, because "What's that noisy old coot hollering for?" is easier, safer, less trouble than thinking about what this explicit statement of censorship as a policy means for your own future mental freedom.

Convergence Culture

HOW DOES THIS RELATE TO NOW, AND HERE?

I joined Goodreads at the behest of a student in 2007. I teach lit. I get a chance daily to read and comment on reading with a circle of smart, engaged readers; I also am supposed to write about my reading, and connect with other readers and writers professionally. Why, I asked this student, would I want to get on a "social networking site for book geeks"? What on earth would be useful — or fun — when my every day is neck-deep in books and writing about books?

Heck, he said, you might find it interesting.

I rambled about for a few weeks. Star ratings and reviews? Amazon has that, and Amazon is a store. Sort of helpful when scanning products, but not much of a resource for a deeper user investment. When I want reviews, I surf about to various (and ever-expanding) professional outlets. What do I get here — what's the value added?

My first inkling of what GR could be was in a rip-roaring fight about Norman Mailer (or it might have been Philip Roth) between David Kowalski, brian gottlieb, and Manny Ramirez. Knuckledusters out — no punches pulled. Mean, uncivil, smart as hell.

I joined in. I realized (small world) that Manny and brian knew someone I knew in L.A. I met, through them, a bunch of other interesting people. It was never so much about their reviews, although good lord David and brian — like so many others on this site — can produce critical reflections as incisive, expansive, downright funny, boldly provocative as anyone writing about literature anywhere ("professional" or not). It was instead about battling, and joining virtual hands, in a bond about books. It was a perfect intersection of critical engagement and community networking ... and I just plain liked the people I ran into, and the chance to read beyond those circles to see how other communities read. (YA — who knew there were such fascinating and invested readers and critical debates? I don't join in, but I have loved being able to examine and relish how invested fans rigorously engage their aesthetic, ethical, personal values over works they cherish or deride.)

But.

It seemed for a stretch that Goodreads had a bead on something wonderful at the corner where the new paradigms of new media are converging. (And here's the hat-tip to Jenkins.) Newspapers are dying, so whither the book review? Well, damn: maybe here? The intersections of the "professional" and the fan review emerge most forcefully — seem most powerfully to build upon what's best in both — when there's a rich social network with an expansive open-access audience. More critics, more writing, more dialogue about literature, more dialogues about the various open contexts which shape literature (the autobiographical, the debates about authors, the connections readers draw between works and with other readers) ... GR had something hot. This isn't a store — see above: Amazon doesn't need a mirror site. But the way this social space could connect to the new marketplace was beyond intriguing — publishing and selling books are also changing radically, and again GR seemed to be finding a way to anchor in READERS' networks and make a new kind of sense of what to publish and how to market. The production and consumption of literature are always linked; GR signaled a possible new kind of linking.

Notice the past tense there? The links between production and consumption, between publishing/selling and a vibrant (finicky, contentious, or in other words INVESTED) audience are always tense. But tension is often a sign of tremendous vitality and health. What *seems* like *Lord of the Flies* (to quote from a recent article) is really just the red-in-tooth-and-claw ecosystem in which literature always thrives. What I think has begun to happen here is an attempt to tamp down the problems, which throws the ecosystem out of whack — which puts the thumb on the scale for producers, corrals the consumers...

... it's what usually happens to vibrant folk cultures when the markets intervene.

Which is probably headier — i.e, pedantic and blowhardier — than is needed. But it seems to me that GR has been tamed, and the taming is a market decision, and I could give a shit about investing in yet another place that is all about me being a *mere* consumer.

A Retelling of Goldilocks

Once upon a time there was a little girl named Goldilocks, who was very interested in online reviewing. She was out in the woods one day, when, walking past a house picturesquely called Bear Cottage, she glanced through the window and happened to notice three books lying on the table. No one seemed to be around, so she opened the door and went in.

She looked at the first book, which was called *Les 120 journées de Sodome ou l'école du libertinage*, by the Marquis de Sade. Not only was it full of the most disgusting descriptions of sexual torture, it was in eighteenth century French! No, no, thought Goldilocks, this book is too hard.

She flicked through the next book, *Princess Daisy*, by Judith Krantz. Apart from a little rape, incest and lesbian action, there was hardly anything to interest a modern girl. No, no, thought Goldilocks, this book is too soft.

She picked up the third book, and found it was *Fifty Shades of Grey*, by E.L. James! Goldilocks had begged to be allowed to read mommyporn, but her mother, a rather strict woman, insisted that she would have to wait until she was ten. Evidently Mrs. Bear was more permissive. Goldilocks quickly posted negative reviews of the first two books on her iPad and settled down to enjoy her new acquisition. She was having such a good time that she didn't even hear the bears come home. Since they immediately went to their laptops, they didn't notice her either. But after a moment, she heard an angry growl from Mr. Bear. "Someone's been off-topic on my book!" he said with a slight French accent.

Mrs. Bear was not far behind. Smarting from the irrelevant insults that Goldilocks had heaped on her favorite writer, she joined her voice to her husband's. "Someone's been off-topic on my book!" she complained bitterly.

Baby Bear looked around for her copy of Fifty Shades, eager to continue with the first bondage scene, but couldn't find it anywhere. Suddenly, looking behind the couch, she found Golilocks not only reading it but also posting flippant updates on Goodreads.

"Someone's been off-topic on *my* book," she yelped, "and she's doing it right now!"

"*Alors*," said Mr. Bear in his French way. "I think you'll just have to *close down her account*".

THE END

Librarian on Strike

I guess I'll start my move with my most "liked" review.

My friends list will be seeing this message a lot over the next days and weeks. Sorry.

I have reviewed this book; the review can be found here, on BookLikes, and here, on my blog. However, I will no longer be posting reviews on Goodreads, due to its recent changes to Terms of Use and, far worse, the boneheaded and incomprehensible way it is proceeding with the new policy. Deleting content, almost randomly, and without warning (whatever they may have said) is wrong. Failing to provide a site-wide announcement is wrong. Failing to address users' very legitimate concern over the situation is wrong.

I'm not going to leave GR while I have good friends remaining here, but I will no longer perform librarian functions, nor will I post anything but links where I used to post reviews.

I will also be posting the gist of this message on my blog, on LibraryThing, on BookLikes, and anywhere else I can think of. And when I review for Netgalley from now on I will state that I no longer post reviews on GR, and why.

It may not affect the situation here — but in good conscience I can't do anything less.

A Review of "Christy"

Until 3 days ago, I had 1500 books on my Goodreads bookshelves. Until one month ago, I was passionate about Goodreads, an evangelist, really, telling everyone I knew — who loves books (and there are a diminishing number of those people in my life, sadly) about the amazing community that I had found here on Goodreads.

This is not a protest review. But it is an off-topic review, although I will get to the point sooner or later.

But I came to Goodreads precisely for the off-topic reviews. For the friendships. For the occasionally over-the-top snark and the silliness and the passion. But mostly because the people that I found here were like *me* in one extremely unique way. There are a lot of people who enjoy reading. There are a lot of people who profess to love books. There are commensurately fewer people who read widely, and wildly, and with a great consuming fury that causes them to recall their lives in books.

I remember that I read *The Portrait of a Lady* on my honeymoon. It was the Penguin classics edition, with the black spine, and I still have it sitting on my bookshelf. I read it next to a pool in Cabo San Lucas, Mexico, and the cover is still rippled where my new husband splashed me in an effort to get me to stop reading and join him at the swim up bar (I did. And this was the first in many years of my husband splashing, poking, tickling, teasing and otherwise attempting to pull my attention away from whatever book I was reading).

I remember that I read *A Game of Thrones* on a cruise. This, too, was in the pre-kindle days, before I could take an entire bookshelf with me everywhere (and what a luxury that turned out to be). I was going away for a week, and I didn't have a lot of space to pack, and cruise ship libraries are, in my experience, pretty bleak places, full of novels written by Nicholas Sparks and little else. In a moment of inspiration, I packed the first three, bricklike paperback editions of

GRRM's epic series, concluding that they would keep me busy for the entire week, while only taking up the space of three paperbacks. I was right. It worked a treat. Except, of course, for the part where I finished the books on the sixth day, leaving me with one lonely, bookless, day to spare.

That is what I found on Goodreads. I found *my people*. People who, when they pack for vacation, pack their books first and decide which clothes to take second, based on how much (little) space is left in the suitcase. People who are always reading, and talking about reading, something.

I have 1100 books on my home kindle account, and another 450 on a bookclub account I share with friends. I have bookshelves full of books at home, at least another four to five hundred books in print form that are waiting for me to read. I could probably read for a full decade and never buy another book (not that I will, but I could.) I am not on Goodreads because I need book recommendations. My entire non-professional brain capacity is given over to books, and authors, and publishers, and random ephemera about all three of them. I can find my own books.

So, what was I here for? I was here for the off-topic. For the stories. For the conversations. For the crazy. For the people who loved, like I did, Trixie Belden. To talk about books that I read long ago and that stole my heart.

Like this one. That is where *Christy* comes into this off-topic review. This is a book that I read long ago, when I was a girl, before I went off to college. It was a library book, that my mother, of all people, checked out because it was a book that she had loved, and she wanted to share it with me.

I wanted to turn up my nose at it — I was a teenager after all, and very, very edgy. And my mother and I were at a rough patch in our relationship. I wore Ray-Ban sunglasses, and skinny jeans with zippers at the ankle, and black (lots and lots of black), I spoke bad high school French. I was insufferable, pretentious, caught up in my own intellect, and I saw little in my mother — doctor's wife, stay-at-home mom — to emulate. God, what a little bitch I was.

And this book was about a Christian girl who goes to Appalachia to teach. There was no reason that this book should have worked for me. And yet, it did. It enraptured me, and I stayed up all night reading it. And even as snotty, and edgy, and obnoxious as I was, I saw the look in my mom's eyes when she asked me if I liked it, and I couldn't lie to her and break her heart, and I admitted that yes, yes I did like it. I liked it a lot, and I thanked her for giving it to me. And we hugged, and some of the tension between myself and my mother, in those very difficult years between childhood and adulthood melted away with that little bit of common ground. From a book. This book.

That's all I have to say.

Except that I'm sad because Goodreads is different now, and this review is off-topic, and off-topic is no longer allowed.

A Review of "1001 Books You Must Read Before You Die"

(licensed by Tracy Mitchel under CC-BY-ND 3.0)

Emily May as a child.

I have never had a problem finding books to read.

My whole life, I've never had a problem finding books to read and love. Of all kinds. Of all genres. I would seek them out, one way or another; they couldn't hide from me. From the Goosebumps books I found lying around on the shared shelves in the classrooms of my first school, to my pretentious swanning around my local library in search of those books called "classics" which meant you were totally smart if you read them (oh yes, I was a real delight as a child). I remember being about seven years old and asking my mum to get me a library card — I checked out the maximum of twelve each time, even though I could only read about one and a half back then before it was time to return them. Once, I even came to my mum in floods of tears because I'd let my books become overdue and thought I was going to prison.

I would even find the books which people had gone to great lengths to hide from me. It's an odd memory that I doubt I'll ever forget. I must have been about eight or nine years old and my family were staying with friends in Holland. The house was beautiful. Huge. And most likely hiding a door that would lead me straight into another world if only I could find it. I stumbled through unused rooms on the third floor like a kid discovering Narnia until I found a box of books. I gravitated towards them. I can't quite tell you why, but Goodreads is the sort of place where I might have a chance of finding someone who understands. I've just always read. I honestly can't remember a time before reading, when books weren't in my life. I don't know if I read as an escape or because of an interest in learning about other people or just to say I could and did. I read everything I could get my hands on. Including the books in this box, which were, shall we say, enlightening. I was appalled — appalled, I tell you! — at the things people are willing to put in their mouths. Needless to say, I read all of the book in question and instinctively never mentioned it to my parents. I'm sure some would like to think of me as a poor wee cherub whose innocence was stolen by evil books — maybe so, but I would put my money on Stine's chicken[25] people being the real culprit rather than a bit of fellatio.

No, I have never had a problem finding books to read.

But I have had a problem finding people who understand what it's like to really LOVE reading. Maybe even need it. People who associate periods of their life with the kinds of things they were reading then, whether in school or in dusty old rooms of a house in Holland. The kind of people who take personal journeys into books and write responses that are part review, part stories in themselves. This is what Goodreads has always given me. It's given me people who've loved a book so much that they've had to tell a story about a specific part of their life — that was the only way they could express the strength of their feeling. It's given me people who write poems for reviews or just post pictures because words aren't enough for what

---

[25] *Chicken Chicken* (Goosebumps #53) by R.L. Stine

they want to say. A lot of these "reviews" don't help me decide whether I'll like a book or not. Many could be considered off-topic, not really about the book in question. And it amuses me how little the Goodreads moderators/managers/whoever actually understand: the books don't really matter.

What Goodreads doesn't seem to understand is that the vast majority of their inactive members who created accounts, rated *Lord of the Flies*, and then quickly left — they came here because they like books. The others, the minority, who provide thousands of reviews, check the site religiously for friend updates, and are under direct attack by the new policies — they came here for the community. For the friends. For the memes. For the poems. For the rants. For the pointlessness. For the off-topic stories. For the ability to express themselves freely.

Goodreads has done a truly fantastic job of not getting it. Of not getting why this site is successful. Goodreads thinks people come to this site for the books; they think they've reinvented the art of finding your next read. Oh, who are they kidding? There are a thousand other books like this and services and unused rooms in Holland that have been helping people find something to read for years. Most of them are quicker and more reliable, and all of them have fewer trolls. No. Goodreads is a long-forgotten URL in the Internet history of millions of people but it means something important to only a few. I came to a site called "Goodreads" because I like books, but it was the people, the wonderful, off-topic people that gave me a reason to stay. You know why I'm still here after all this time? It's not the fucking books. It's the heartfelt expressions of utter delight and rage in the "reviews" of the friends I've made. Or it's the funny memes they post and the pictures of their cats. Or it's that teenage girl who emailed me after reading my pretty damn off-topic review of *This Song Will Save Your Life*[26] and said she was going through the same thing but my review gave her encouragement to make it through each day.

---

[26]*This Song Will Save Your Life* by Leila Sales

Goodreads, I don't need your help finding books to read.

I can feel this site losing its value bit by bit. With every creative, talented and interesting person that leaves, Goodreads loses more of my interest. I can honestly feel my interest waning each day. I used to keep Goodreads open in a permanent tab that I would refresh a ridiculous number of times so I didn't miss anything. Now? I'm bored. This site now has more books than ever before and I'm bored. Because it was everything off-topic about Goodreads that gave the site its worth. I can find books elsewhere. Easily. Without issue. I've been doing it my whole life.

This is not a protest review. For one thing, that would imply that I expect or hope it to have some kind of effect — I don't. This is not a review at all, actually. This is just a post of my thoughts for people to take as they wish. As I've always done on Goodreads and as I will continue to do. I'd say I don't care if someone deletes this, but that would be a lie. Because every deleted "review" is another piece of something I love being chipped away.

One Foot Out The Door

So, there's been some really ugly shit going down the last few weeks.

I have been watching this develop from the first time someone brought the feedback thread to my attention on that sneaky Friday this all happened. I have been lurking around the edges as the narrative developed, moving from one well-timed, national-press noticed review to a continuing stream of thoughtful challenges to Goodreads' new, still not site-wide announced ToU.

I have many, many friends and acquaintances on this site who have been stating their case against Goodreads' shockingly ill-advised and ill-publicized decision regarding their ToU from the very beginning. Ceridwen has done an awe-inspiring amount of work crunching the numbers and researching the extent of the site's folly. Elizabeth wrote an incredibly saddening and clear statement about why she will no longer review on the site. The Hydra Principle was started by Manny and has been ably followed and articulated and amplified by Mariel, Jennifer and a great many other people. Moira just said goodbye. Others have been very vocal in commenting, flagging, changing their usernames to signal their support, and keeping the all-important feedback thread going, despite Goodreads' attempts to continuously ignore its existence.

I've been watching it all and I have been moved, saddened, angered and, it must be said, proud to see all the work that these amazing people have done.

Me? Well. I'm a little ashamed. Other than liking updates, religiously following along and reading and waiting ... I've been mostly a silent, quiet supporter of all of this, following the lead of my braver, more articulate friends and fellows.

I just ... I don't know how to explain why except to say that I often feel, in an argument, that I spend more time thinking about all the ways that I must be wrong because someone else must know better than me. I am used to deferring to authority for the most part —

largely in the interest of being left alone to do my quiet, hiding-in-books-and-writing thing in the hope that it that it wasn't as big a thing as I thought, emotionally, that it was (that's usually the way it turns out).

I also have six and a half years of vested interest in hoping that it does just that, to go along with my own personal inclination. You guys, I have been on this site longer than I have known my husband (years longer than we have been married). I have been on this site longer than I was in college (undergrad and both graduate degrees included). Longer than most of the hobbies I have had and dropped in my life. Longer than I waited for that fucking ASOIAF book, people. It's ... a very big part of my life. I have found a place where I will not be ridiculed for going on for hours about how much I love Tolstoy, and where I will find other people willing to expend just as much energy expressing their anger about poorly written romance novels. I have found a place where I can spend as many hours as I like discussing Jane Austen books and then do it again the next day — and re-read the novels three times and still find someone who will talk about the latest thing I found with me. I have found a community of people whose reviews I can turn to on bad days to make me laugh and move me with beauty. I know on any given day there will be a dozen books I want to add to my ever-growing to-read pile and just as many people to commiserate with about never reaching the end of it. This bibliophilia ... it's a lifestyle of sorts that it is sometimes hard to find support for once you have reached an adult age, unless you are fortunate enough to be paid for what you do. To find not only a place for books and readers, but a virtual neighborhood with community gathering spaces ... words fail me when I try to describe what it has meant to me. This site has been a wonderful refuge, haven, exploring ground ... so many things, that has helped see me through my transition out of college and into a wider world as I figured out who I was and what I wanted.

Ceridwen recently did a radio interview in which she stated that Goodreads had changed her life. I laughed aloud with joy when

I heard that because I felt exactly the same. I recently decided to change my medium-term career plans based on the joy I have found here in reading, reviewing, and especially writing. This is something I have been brave enough to do based on the constant support of the community here. Nobody here knows it, but if you are reading this, you were a part of that, and I can't thank you enough for your generosity, your intelligence, your kindness, your brilliant analytic minds and your wonderful senses of humor.

And that ... in a nutshell is why I have been hiding my head in the sand, hoping that this was all some horrible mistake, and it would all go away. That this was the work of some lone, overworked community manager who was trying to apply the fastest solution to a problem that would get her out the door on a Friday, and which she would strongly rethink on Monday. That somehow the higher management didn't know about it, and while it remained within reasonable grounds, didn't need to know about it. Or maybe there was some argument to be made for civility, however badly expressed — surely someone would come along and refine the statement so it made more sense? Surely the apology was coming? There was no way that Goodreads was actually going to sit back and let the perception be that it was only deleting negative reviews and supporting an all-positive-buy-books model.

Right?

Right?

One week went by ... Two weeks went by ... incredibly THREE WEEKS WENT BY and ... nothing.

And then they started deleting the protest reviews.

That was my line. When they started to stamp out dissent, actually to make it disappear with virtually no excuse for doing so ... That's not neglect. That's not an overwhelmed person or people trying to figure it out. That's an entity that has decided that they do not care, that they have moved on from the issue, do not see it as an issue, and is trying to avoid bad press. Or they are too far down the line to backtrack on what they've been doing and save face. They're content with their wildly inconsistent policy enough to no longer care what effect it is having on their user base. If you try to silence dissent, then something is very, very wrong.

This is not the site I joined back in 2007. I can't tell you how laissez-faire this site has been since then — I have never once had anything in my reviews interfered with, nor even the suggestion of doing so, despite posting negative reviews, despite posting reviews that spoke directly about the author, with some less than kind remarks. The administration was invisible (other than popping in on some threads personally in the very, very early days to talk about books), for all I knew. And I thought the user base largely ran itself very well under those circumstances.

It is just so easy to see that it did not have to be like this. There were and are so many other ways they could have handled this, many better ways to even try to begin figuring out this mess. And again, this is me, the person with no social skills, the little quiet book mouse in the corner, speaking.

Look ... and I can't even begin to tell you how true this is ... I am not the person who pushes back. Not even, sometimes, about stuff like this where I should. I am not the person who kicks and yells and fights. I am usually convinced that I am wrong, even if I am not. I am not the person you ever expect to say a goddamn thing in the meeting.

And ME, THAT PERSON, I am saying more than one or two goddamn things about this.

And I am not the only person like me doing so.

You might want to consider that.

I can't lie, you made it personal by fucking with my friends and my community. My friends are leaving. My friends are crying. My friends are deleting their profiles and their hard work and moving elsewhere. My friends who draw an amazing amount of traffic and discussion and who get good publicity for this site. I might be quiet and I am certain that I would have a very small effect if I left this site, but they won't and they don't deserve you treating them this way after all their work — nobody does and I am pissed for the community in general, but they are the ones that I will get pissed about today because again, you fucked with my friends.

The community is the reason that so many of us are here, I think, and not on our own blogs alone somewhere in the cybersphere, the reason that many of us come back and keep writing when otherwise I think ... well I can't speak for anyone else, but there were times when I almost gave up on reviewing, but I was always drawn back in by some vibrant discussion or some amazing book that I just had to be a part of reading. And your decisions are fucking with that community.

I haven't made a final decision on what to do other than 1) creating a BookLikes account and getting ready to jump ship if need be, if this awful trend continues without any correction by Goodreads and 2) not creating any new book reviews for Goodreads in the future. I am still deciding whether to delete my reviews entirely. For the time being, I am leaving my profile intact in one last foolish hope that Goodreads will see reason and figure this horrible mess out.

It's heartbreaking to even contemplate leaving but to be honest ... if my community leaves, then Goodreads doesn't exist in any real way for me anymore. And that's that.

I am continuing to lurk here for now and hope, but I am fast thinking it only a fool's hope.

If you are leaving, dear friends, please let me know where you are going. I want to keep my community intact, even if Goodreads can't be the place where that happens anymore.

Part VIII

But what is censorship?

What conclusions can we draw from this as yet unfinished story? Themis-Athena ponders how the draftsmen of the United States' foundational documents, many of whom were lawyers — and all of them, astute and far-seeing leaders — might view some of the issues associated with recent events, had they been around to watch them unfold. Notgettingenough, going back to basics, argues that no one is obviously in the right, and that the very notions of "free speech" and "censorship" are poorly defined. Everyone has trouble making their own voice heard, and everyone, at least to some extent, restricts others in trying to make their voices heard. She exhorts readers to speak up for what they actually believe in, irrespective of what it may happen to be.

Perhaps only one lesson is clear: surprisingly many people dislike arbitrary use of authority, and will react strongly against it even in apparently trivial cases.

What the Founding Fathers Might Have Said to Each Other About Censorship on Goodreads

In Heaven

[BENJAMIN FRANKLIN is looking at a computer screen showing the Goodreads logo and a review with a Hydra image at the top. Other Founding Fathers approach, looking over his shoulder.]

PATRICK HENRY: Still hung up on life on Earth, Mr. Franklin? You really should let it go, you know. After all these centuries...

FRANKLIN: How can I? It's endlessly fascinating. Humanity is, you know.

JAMES MADISON: But that thing you're holding is just one of those new computer machines they have now. I understand that you would find it interesting as an engineer — but nothing to do with humanity, surely?

FRANKLIN: On the contrary. It has everything to do with humanity. You see, this computer allows humans to communicate in a virtual space — leaving behind the physical world...

THOMAS JEFFERSON *[grinning]*: ... a bit like us, these days, then...

FRANKLIN: ... although if they connect this computer to a printer, they can still print out the virtual exchange and bring it back into the physical world.

MADISON *[aside, to JEFFERSON]*: I had a feeling the printing business would come into it somewhere.

HENRY, to FRANKLIN: And?

FRANKLIN: Well, and in that virtual space people now congregate just as they do in the physical world. They form clubs, societies, discussion forums...

HENRY: Ah. And I suppose that virtual space has a government that doesn't like some of those discussions. Or the physical world's government interferes and tries to suppress them. Or some such thing. Give me liberty or give me death![27]

ALEXANDER HAMILTON: That line is so 1798 ...[28]

HENRY: You should talk — you didn't die for anybody's liberty.

HAMILTON: I did indeed, Sir, for the liberty to speak my mind!

AARON BURR *[approaching]*: To slander a man's reputation, you mean, Sir.

HAMILTON: What is he doing here? Have they opened up the gates of Hell? Get him out of my sight!

[GEORGE WASHINGTON and JOHN ADAMS gently but firmly lead BURR away again.]

MADISON: Isn't this a moot point anyway? If we are not talking about the real world, we can hardly be speaking about death, can we?

FRANKLIN: But about liberty. Free speech, especially. And as I am sure we all agree, whoever would overthrow the liberty of a nation must begin by subduing the freeness of speech.[29]

MADISON: Well, we are hardly talking about nations, either, here. Or are we?

FRANKLIN *[shrugging]*: Society, then. Surely you would agree that people do not suddenly change their character and their behavior when they start communicating with each other in a virtual space. They will still want to express their ideas and opinions — freely trade their ideas within the competition of the market, if you will. Thus, a discussion taking place in a virtual space is as much a

---

[27] http://en.wikipedia.org/wiki/Give_me_liberty,_or_give_me_death!

[28] Patrick Henry died in 1799.

[29] *Silence Dogood* No. 8, July 9, 1722, contained in *Franklin: Writings* (Library of America), J.A. Leo Lemay (ed.), p. 24

discussion in the market place of ideas as a discussion in the physical world.[30]

JEFFERSON *[nodding]*: Where the best course of action, even towards opinions with which we violently disagree, is always to let them stand undisturbed as monuments of the safety with which error of opinion may be tolerated, where reason is left free to combat it. Yes.[31]

ADAMS: Excuse me, but I'm afraid I still don't quite understand how this virtual space works. Surely once an opinion, or a statement, is transmitted into this virtual space, it doesn't just float around there. It has to go somewhere specific — there actually has to be some sort of virtual equivalent to a marketplace for all this to make sense. How are these discussion forums that you mentioned created, Mr. Franklin?

FRANKLIN: Well, essentially someone — this can be anyone, an individual, a company, whoever — registers what is called a virtual domain and, in that domain, creates a space where the actual exchange of opinions then takes place — they're calling that a website. The one I am looking at, for example, is all about books; it's called Goodreads.

JEFFERSON: Registering a domain — like staking a claim in pre-

---

[30]The first U.S. Supreme Court opinion referencing the notion of a marketplace, or a free trade of ideas was *Abrams v. U.S.*, 250 U.S. 616 (1919) (see http://caselaw.lp.findlaw.com/scripts/getcase.pl?navby=case&court=us&vol=250&page=616), where that description appears as part of Justice Oliver Wendell Holmes Jr.'s dissent. It became a staple of appellate U.S. First Amendment case law after having been centrally relied on by Justice William O. Douglas in his concurring opinion in *United States v. Rumely*, 345 U.S. 41 (1953) (see http://caselaw.lp.findlaw.com/scripts/getcase.pl?navby=case&court=us&vol=345&page=41\#), a case that upheld, on First Amendment grounds, the right of individuals and organizations to refuse to divulge to the government the identity and particulars of the members/subscribers to an organization critical of the government.

[31]First Inaugural Address, March 4, 1801, in: *Jefferson, Writings* (Library of America), Merrill D. Peterson (ed.), p. 493.

viously uninhabited land, you mean; say, the way it was done in Oklahoma or Ohio when we were around and in the century after us?

FRANKLIN: The principle would appear to be similar, yes.

ADAMS: But then, if this can be done by private individuals, surely any of them can, and will, want to set their own rules of behavior in their own house ... or 'domain.' Why should this be different? I mean to say, the freedom of speech that we fought for and wrote into the First Amendment is a protection against an intrusive government ... but all of us would surely still want to set rules for our own household and expect those to be obeyed, wouldn't we?

FRANKLIN: Maybe so, but this is a house into which people are being invited specifically with the idea of an exchange of opinions in mind. How are you going to create a viable marketplace of opinions in any environment if you preordain what people may and what they may not talk about?

ADAMS: But surely even in such an environment some rules are necessary — without them, any society, or any group, would just disintegrate into chaos. Think of hate speech, libel and slander, for example ...

[HAMILTON frowns.]

THOMAS PAINE: If, to expose the fraud and imposition of monarchy ... to promote universal peace, civilization, and commerce, and to break the chains of political superstition, and raise degraded man to his proper rank; if these things be libellous ... let the name of libeller be engraved on my tomb.[32]

MADISON: Hmm. An important point, Mr. Paine. The question of definition — of the labels we attach to something. How does one define 'permissible' speech — for lack of a better word — in such an environment then? On that Goodreads website, for example, that you mentioned, Mr. Franklin ... I assume there will be some rules

---

[32] *Letter Addressed To The Addressers On The Late Proclamation* (summer 1792), in Michael Foot, Isaac Kramnick (eds.), *The Thomas Paine Reader*, p. 374.

about what types of contributions they do not wish to see. How is this being handled there?

JEFFERSON: And are those rules being applied evenly? I have to say that I do find the mere notion of regulating speech quite galling, even in a private environment, but at the very least, if there is such a thing at all, there should be a perception of equity and fairness.

ADAMS [*muttering*]: Hear, hear. The expert on avoiding double standards. Say, dear Sir, how *is* Sally Hemings these days?

ABIGAIL ADAMS [*from a distance*]: Now, John ...

FRANKLIN: Well, in what they call their Terms of Use,[33] they prohibit content that constitutes a crime or a tort. That's to be expected, I should think. They also say, however, for example, that by making use of their service, users agree — and I quote — 'not to post User Content that may create a risk of emotional distress to any animal ...'

[*The Founding Fathers exchange puzzled looks.*]

FRANKLIN: ... or content that, quote, 'contains any information or content that we deem to be profane, or otherwise objectionable' — 'we' is the company that owns the website, of course.

MADISON [*nonplussed*]: Users agree not to post anything that *they divine* the owners may subsequently deem objectionable?

JEFFERSON [*nodding*]: And coming back to Mr. Madison's earlier point — and never mind whether what is profanity to me may or may not also be profanity to any of you gentlemen, or to these Goodreads people — is at least that term 'otherwise objectionable' defined anywhere?

FRANKLIN: If it is, I have not found that place, yet.

ADAMS: But that is not sound ...

[*PAINE and HENRY snort.*]

ADAMS: I mean to say, how can you even begin trying to enforce

---

[33]https://www.goodreads.com/about/terms

such terms? Fairly and equitably, at that?

MADISON: How indeed.

ADAMS: Out of interest, where is this all taking place — where is the domicile of that Goodreads company that created this website?

FRANKLIN: California.

HAMILTON *[groaning]*: They should've left that place to the Mexicans ...

WASHINGTON: I wouldn't say that, Alexander — strategically even of supreme importance, I'd have thought. Access to the Pacific Ocean alone, never mind its natural resources ...

ADAMS *[pulling out a sheaf of notes]*: Wait a moment.

JEFFERSON: Still following how the law on Earth is evolving, dear Sir?

ADAMS *[reading]*: Yes — here it is ... this seems to come up rather frequently, so I'm just going to read a bit from one decision by the Ninth Circuit Court of Appeals[34] — that's the one for California

---

[34]*Davis v. O'Melveny & Myers*, 9th Cir. No. 04-56039, argued and submitted March 7, 2006; opinion of May 14, 2007 (see http://caselaw.findlaw.com/us-9th-circuit/1043333.html), citing, inter alia:

Nagrampa v. MailCoups, Inc., 469 F.3d 1257 (9th Cir.2006) (en banc; see http://caselaw.findlaw.com/us-9th-circuit/1491498.html);

Armendariz v. Found. Health Psychcare Servs., Inc., 24 Cal.4th 83, 99 Cal.Rptr.2d 745, 6 P.3d 669 (2000) (see http://caselaw.findlaw.com/ca-supreme-court/1130714.html);

Soltani v. W. & S. Life Ins. Co., 258 F.3d 1038, 1042 (9th Cir.2001) (see http://caselaw.findlaw.com/us-9th-circuit/1301529.html);

Szetela v. Discover Bank, 97 Cal.App.4th 1094, 118 Cal.Rptr.2d 862 (2002) (see http://caselaw.findlaw.com/ca-court-of-appeal/1076052.html);

Ferguson v. Countrywide Credit Industries, Inc., 298 F.3d 778 (9th Cir.2002) (see http://caselaw.findlaw.com/us-9th-circuit/1260590.html);

Ingle v. Circuit City Stores, Inc., 328 F.3d 1165 (9th Cir.2003) ("Ingle I") (see http://caselaw.findlaw.com/us-9th-circuit/1136919.html);

and the other Pacific states ...

JEFFERSON, MADISON, HAMILTON and HENRY *[unisono]*: We know.

ADAMS: So as I was going to say, this decision would appear to sum up the relevant issues. It holds, in pertinent part: 'Under California law, a contractual clause is unenforceable if it is both procedurally and substantively unconscionable. Courts apply a sliding scale: the more substantively oppressive the contract term, the less evidence of procedural unconscionability is required to come to the conclusion that the term is unenforceable, and vice versa.

In assessing *procedural* unconscionability, the court focuses on whether the contract was one of adhesion ... Was there an opportunity to negotiate? The test focuses on factors of oppression and surprise. ... Whether the plaintiff had an opportunity to decline the defendant's contract and instead enter into a contract with another party that does not include the offending terms is not the relevant test for procedural unconscionability ... [The applicable case law] has rejected the notion that the availability in the marketplace of substitute goods or services alone can defeat a claim of procedural unconscionability. ... Where [one party to the contract] is facing an[other party] with overwhelming bargaining power that drafted the contract, and presented it to [the first party] on a take-it-or-leave-it basis, the clause is procedurally unconscionable.

Substantive unconscionability relates to the effect of the contract or provision. A lack of mutuality is relevant in analyzing this prong. The term focuses on the terms of the agreement and whether those terms are so one-sided as to shock the conscience. A determination of substantive unconscionability involves whether the terms of the

---

Morris v. Redwood Empire Bancorp, 128 Cal.App.4th 1305, 27 Cal.Rptr.3d 797 (2005) (see `http://caselaw.findlaw.com/ca-court-of-appeal/1448012.html`);

Circuit City Stores, Inc. v. Adams, 279 F.3d 889 (9th Cir.2002) (on remand)(see `http://caselaw.findlaw.com/us-9th-circuit/1233073.html`).

contract are unduly harsh or oppressive ... [When the construction of a contractual clause is at issue], the concern is ... with the scope of the language.'

MADISON: Am I correct in assuming the Goodreads Terms of Use are unilaterally drafted by this Goodreads company?

FRANKLIN: That would be the case, yes.

MADISON: And the average Goodreads user — would their bargaining power be equal to that of the company ... equal financial means, equal access to legal advice, etc.?

FRANKLIN: Goodreads is a service being used by several million subscribers worldwide, so — no, that strikes me as highly unlikely.

MADISON: How are the Goodreads Terms of Use communicated?

FRANKLIN: They are posted on a designated page of the website.

HAMILTON: Hardly surprising, then.

MADISON: But I suppose by signing up with the service you are deemed to have agreed to the terms? It's essentially 'take it or leave it'?

FRANKLIN: Indeed, so the Terms of Use expressly state.

MADISON: A contract of adhesion, surely, then. No free negotiation whatsoever. And the case law which Mr. Adams just referenced holds that the freedom not to use this particular service but choose that of another, similar company does not make any difference.

JEFFERSON: But not every contract of adhesion is unconscionable, and therefore unenforceable.

ADAMS: No, but surely one can only marvel at that 'otherwise objectionable' language.

MADISON: Particularly in light of the fact that users themselves are essentially charged with divining whether Goodreads will find their content 'otherwise objectionable' ...

JEFFERSON: What happens if a user is found to be in violation of the Terms of Use — say for having submitted content that Goodreads finds 'profane' or 'otherwise objectionable', for whatever reason?

FRANKLIN: On this, the Terms of Use state that, quote, 'Goodreads may permanently or temporarily terminate, suspend, or otherwise refuse to permit your access to the Service without notice and liability for any reason, including if in Goodreads's sole determination you violate any provision of this Agreement, or for no reason.'

HAMILTON: So it's a contract at will. Nothing illegal in that, as far as I'm aware.

MADISON: Well, not as such, but there does seem to be an arbitrary balance in favor of these Goodreads gentlemen — especially if you look at the way in which the adhesive nature of the terms, and that vague language we've been discussing, and the power to terminate the user's rights in Goodreads's 'sole determination' play together. And I must say on the whole my conscience finds this all pretty shocking, to use the happy phrase you quoted from that opinion, Mr. Adams.

JEFFERSON: Yes, one has to wonder, doesn't one: can one party to a contract compel another to accept that contract to be framed as 'at will' by way of a contract of adhesion — isn't that a contradiction in terms? Can one party force the other party to accept the right to terminate the contract at will just because it's being framed as a mutual right — doesn't that defeat the contract's very purpose? At least if the contract's very existence is premised on the notion of participation in the first place ...

HAMILTON: Well, this isn't exactly Rousseau's *Social Contract*, you know.

WASHINGTON *[shaking his head, frowning]*: Never mind the niceties of that case law on which you legal gentlemen are always getting so hung up: Why would any business want to behave in this manner in the first place — first invite people in and let them believe they are going to be able to have a good old chinwag about just about anything they please, and then throw them out again for no good reason whatever ... or who knows, for having just such a chinwag? Mr. Franklin, I understood you to say this is a business with several million subscribers worldwide. Surely that size did not come overnight. How could they have grown to even a fraction of that size, I wonder, if they are showing this type of erratic behavior? It does not sound like solid policy to me at all.

JEFFERSON *[nodding]*: Prudence, indeed, will dictate that Governments long established should not be changed for light and transient causes.[35]

FRANKLIN: Still true in every particular, that document, yes. I've been following this story for quite a while now, however ...

MADISON *[aside]*: The old newspaper man again ...

FRANKLIN: ... and it would appear that there recently has in fact been a rather drastic change of policy. As far as I can determine, application of the Terms of Use was initially very restrained. Indeed, the former owner of the business even agreed, not so long ago, that by deleting user content, and again I quote, 'whenever we feel like it, that we've gone down a censorship road that doesn't take us to a good place.'

HENRY and PAINE: Well said, Mr. Owner, whosoever you are.

WASHINGTON *[simultaneously]*: The *former* owner?

FRANKLIN: Yes. The business was sold a few months ago, to an even larger worldwide company.

HAMILTON: This marketplace of book opinions must be a very lucrative thing then. I venture a guess that the buyer is in the literature business as well?

FRANKLIN: They are a large international seller of ... well, initially mostly books and such, I understand, but these days, really every sort of product. In the book area, they've created a special sort of computer that allows people to read books right on their computer

---

[35]The full text of the Declaration of Independence can be found, inter alia, at http://www.archives.gov/exhibits/charters/declaration_transcript.html

screen — no bound and printed pages involved any longer at all.

ADAMS: How disappointing. Those are no books at all, I do not think I would like those things. They probably don't even smell like real books, I mean, no smell of ink, and leather or cardboard or musty paper — not to speak of their look and touch ... the pleasure of actually handling the book as you are reading and turning the pages ...

FRANKLIN: They are hugely popular, however. They've also made it very easy for aspiring writers to get published. All they need to do now is feed their manuscripts into the services offered by this company — they are called Amazon — and from there anybody can then download their books into these new reading computers.

JEFFERSON: Well, I suppose there goes editorial control and minimum quality standards in writing then.

HAMILTON: Oh, but I see, and since this is all happening in the world of computers, there is probably a way to link that exchange on this Goodreads website into those new reading machines as well, isn't there?

FRANKLIN: There is, and I understand this was in fact the chief motive in acquiring the company.

HAMILTON [nodding]: Absolutely. The marketing potential is enormous.

JEFFERSON: But so is the conflict of interest. An owner like this will always put selling first — and the interests of the authors using its services to promote their books. What happens if someone dislikes a book and says so on that Goodreads website?

FRANKLIN: Yes, that is precisely how the conflict emerged. Authors started to complain about what they called unfair reviews — bad reviews, which occasionally also pointed out that the authors were engaging in unethical marketing methods, such as reviewing their own books under assumed false identities and outright buying favorable reviews — which I understand is something that has been going on on Amazon's own website for quite a while. Large newspapers like the New York Times[36] and Forbes[37] have written about it — Forbes even called the practice 'Amazon's Rotten Core';[38] there have been studies by universities like Yale[39] and Cornell[40] ... both rather prominent places these days, incidentally ... and the New York State Attorney General[41] has started to initiate prosecutions of these people.

ADAMS: As well he should. Such methods are fraud, nothing less.

FRANKLIN: Well, it would appear that Amazon and Goodreads have determined it to be in their best interest to believe the authors who deny having committed this type of fraud, and who complain about what they see as 'bad' reviews. So Goodreads determined in the interest of 'setting an appropriate tone' that comments about authors were no longer permissible.[42]

PAINE: But this is lunacy. It's a place for the discussion of literature. How can authors not be relevant to that discussion?

JEFFERSON: Exactly. If I read an article written by Mr. Hamilton here damning that man Burr to Hell and back ...

HAMILTON: *Will* you please refrain from mentioning that name in my presence, Sir.

---

[36] http://www.nytimes.com/2012/08/26/business/book-reviewers-for-hire-meet-a-demand-for-online-raves.html?_r=0

[37] http://www.forbes.com/sites/suwcharmananderson/2012/08/28/fake-reviews-amazons-rotten-core/

[38] http://www.forbes.com/sites/suwcharmananderson/2012/08/28/fake-reviews-amazons-rotten-core/

[39] http://faculty.som.yale.edu/dinamayzlin/EffectWOMSalesdraftSep26.pdf

[40] http://aclweb.org/anthology/P/P11/P11-1032.pdf; http://www.freelunch.me/

[41] http://www.nytimes.com/2013/09/23/technology/give-yourself-4-stars-online-it-might-cost-you.html

[42] https://www.goodreads.com/topic/show/1499741-important-note-regarding-reviews

JEFFERSON: ... shouldn't I also have a chance to find out that the two gentlemen have been engaged in a personal feud practically ever since they first ran into each other?

HAMILTON: Every word I have ever written about him is the unmitigated truth.

JEFFERSON: So you may believe. He calls it slander.

WASHINGTON: The point, Alexander, is that the owner of the business must decide whether to try and arbitrate such a situation or stay out of it. And an owner who is in the business of selling books cannot be expected to be recognized as a fair arbitrator — I quite agree with Mr. Jefferson on that. There will always be a perception of partiality in favor of the authors ... of a bias in favor of sales.

FRANKLIN: Especially if content is being struck immediately once the changed approach has been agreed upon, without any prior notice to the users at all, as happened here.

MADISON [*incredulous*]: I beg your pardon? — How unbelievably ill-advised.

HENRY: Outrageous ...

PAINE: Staggering.

FRANKLIN: And speaking of ownership, there actually is yet another aspect to the issue, as Goodreads has invited its reader-users in not only to discuss books, but also to curate that website — to maintain its virtual catalogue of books current and correct, and perform other tasks that would fall to a librarian in the physical world. Indeed, they are calling the users who volunteer for this work — without any compensation, incidentally — 'librarians.' And by investing a substantial part of their free time into the site, users — librarians especially — have come to actually consider it *their* website. Not in the sense of legal ownership, of course, but in the sense that this is a place and a community, albeit a virtual one, that they deeply care about and are invested in every way *but* as legal owners.

JEFFERSON: Well, then it strikes me that there is really only one thing they can do. *[Reminiscent]* 'We hold these truths to be self-evident, that all men are created equal, that they are endowed by their Creator with certain unalienable Rights, that among these are Life, Liberty and the pursuit of Happiness ... That whenever any Form of Government becomes destructive of these ends, it is the Right of the People to alter or to abolish it, and to institute new Government, laying its foundation on such principles and organizing its powers in such form, as to them shall seem most likely to effect their Safety and Happiness ... ' [43]

PAINE: Hear, hear.

WASHINGTON *[amused]*: A virtual revolution. And how would you stage that, Mr. Jefferson?

FRANKLIN: I can tell you how it was in fact staged, General ... Mr. President.

WASHINGTON: Oh?

FRANKLIN: Yes, you see, that is where this Hydra image here on the screen becomes relevant. One of the website's best-known reviewers — I think I'm very much going to enjoy meeting him some day, as a matter of fact — convinced a group of his friends to replicate every censored review and preface it with this Hydra image, to symbolize that whenever reviewer content was removed, the same content would come back two- and threefold. The practice spread like wildfire. In addition, reviewers took to submitting what they called protest reviews, which purposely broke every rule in the Terms of Use in order to show the arbitrariness of their wording and application. Soon the administrators of the site had their hands full deleting things right, left and center; especially since users also expressly 'flagged' each others' reviews as a violation of the terms — flagging brings content to the attention of the website's administra-

---

[43]The full text of the Declaration of Independence can be found, inter alia, at http://www.archives.gov/exhibits/charters/declaration_transcript.html.

tors, you see. Ultimately, when they could find no other grounds for deletion, Goodreads just labeled such reviews as 'off topic' and removed them on those grounds. And pray do not ask me what 'off topic' is even intended to refer to, because I cannot make head nor tail of it, either.

ADAMS: Well, I assume they would include it in the description of 'otherwise objectionable' ...

MADISON: It is certainly on the same level of specificity. Or rather, lack thereof.

WASHINGTON: And we all know first hand where that sort of action leads in the physical world.

HENRY *[nodding]*: Give me liberty or give me death! I knew the sentiment had to come in somewhere.

WASHINGTON: Except that you really cannot kill someone in that virtual space they have nowadays. Surely that is still something that can only happen in the physical world.

FRANKLIN: I wouldn't say that — as a matter of fact, you can wipe out someone's existence in the virtual world even more easily than in the physical world. You see, all the administrator of a website needs to do is delete their account from the website — or if they come back and open a new account, ultimately by blocking the computers they are using to access the site. And several of the 'Hydra' users have indeed been threatened with the removal of their accounts, I understand.

MADISON: Which, in the words of that original owner of the business, would mean that they now really have 'gone down a censorship road that doesn't take them to a good place.'[44] Well, such a road wouldn't take them anywhere else, would it? It simply can't.

FRANKLIN: No, indeed not. Whoever would overthrow the liberty of a nation must begin by subduing the freeness of speech. I rather regret what is becoming of this Goodreads website — I will not hold

---

[44]cf. p. iii

back from you that I quite used to enjoy it myself ... not only for the very useful information about the tens of thousands of books that have been published since our time — you would be astonished, I assure you, gentlemen — but just for the sort of allegedly 'off topic' commentary that is now prohibited. But there it is ...

ABIGAIL ADAMS *[joining the group]*: And what is becoming of the reviewers who feel they are no longer wanted?

FRANKLIN: Oh, many of them have since decamped to a similar, newer website called BookLikes. It's a bit like the Pilgrim Fathers' Massachusetts and Virginia colonies — very much under construction still — but by and large, they sound like they are quite happy there. As were our ancestors in the early days of the colonies ...

HAMILTON: Well, what happens when this new website becomes too large to be run on a small budget, as I assume it currently is — or such an interesting target that this Amazon business, or some company like Amazon, will want to acquire it in turn? That would appear to be the catch, wouldn't it? Either stay small and only marginally profitable, but "fly under the radar" and be able to foster an environment where readers can have the discussion they want. Or become large and attractive, but thereby also attract the attention of a potential buyer who will turn the business model on its head. The one may be preferable from the users' point of view, the other, undoubtedly, from the owner's. How will that conflict be resolved?

FRANKLIN *[smiling]*: Well, in theory there is a third option, of course: they could also become large and successful enough to be able to rule their world — their business environment — themselves, as our country has become ... well, in a manner of speaking at least. But the future does have some of those 'burned' reviewers worried, and I cannot blame them. And who knows, maybe the only long-term solution really is going to be to bring legal ownership and — shall we call it emotional ownership — together. Interesting times down on earth, gentlemen, in any event. I wouldn't miss watching them for anything in the world. And I am sure if we were still around we'd be able to lend a bit of a hand ...

WASHINGTON: A toast to that. You, angel — a round of nectar and some ambrosia for these brave gentlemen and myself! *[Looking at MRS. ADAMS]* And for the lady, of course!

A Review of "Fair Play or Foul" by its author

Censorship is like bacteria, or those tiny little mites that live on each of us in their millions without us being conscious of them. We are surrounded by censorship, we all live by and through it, every day we exercise it ourselves and experience the censorship of others. From the time we begin to learn to speak we are told and told and told what we can't say. We find out that speech is anything but free and we so quickly take it for granted and learn how to operate within the context of free speech that isn't free, that maybe we never think about the ramifications of that at all.

If you have reached this part of the book, you might be thinking 'wow, all those people just saying what they think because hey, that's free speech isn't it?' And if you thought that, you couldn't be more wrong. The pieces in this book are a result of a complex process of censorship. They have been through self-censorship "hmmm. I'd like to say Manny's a dick-head, but maybe not ... '. They've had the John-Grisham-reader's censorship. 'Hey, you can't say Manny's a dick-head, I'm sure that must be slander ... ' and they've been through copy-editing censorship — 'yeah, I know you want to say dick-head, but take my word for it, there is no hyphen in dickhead. I don't care if you think this is a violation of your free speech rights.' There has been censorship in totality — 'I'm sorry, this is a great piece about Manny being a dickhead, but if you read the requirements for submission, this is a book about his not being a dickhead ... yes, we understand what you are saying, but no, we don't think we need a piece for balance.' This is something editors have to do, they are the last step in the process. Then there is censorship by disagreement. 'If you say Manny's a dickhead, I'm withdrawing my piece.' There has certainly been some of that in the growth of this book too. I, for one, have said at various times 'If that goes in, my piece is out.' In my case this has been about pictorial content that I have found objectionable.

The following piece has been censored by this last consideration.

What happens when somebody makes such a statement 'it's me or her?' What happens next? We take it for granted that free speech is a right without ever thinking about it until it impinges on our feelings, our territory, our comfort zone. Then it becomes hard. On Goodreads, for example, I try not to delete comments on the basis of their offensiveness, but occasionally I do. Other people are less restrictive than that ... or more.

My piece as it was originally presented was strongly opposed by one of the contributors, leading to a rather traumatic period where the whole issue of free speech naturally came under the magnifying glass. In fact, somewhat to their shock, this person discovered that maybe they weren't in favour of free speech after all, not unqualified no holds barred free speech. Having realised that and writing to me that maybe there are things more important than free speech has had me thinking too. Yes, there may be things more important than free speech. Maybe sometimes civility is more important. Maybe even if I was right, being right isn't the most important thing. Maybe letting somebody else have their way is more important.

I say maybe, because I don't really know. I have done very little else for the last month than talk about free speech and censorship, read about it, argue about it. At night as we are settling into bed, I'm afraid it has become foreplay. As usual when I say my most serious things, people will probably think it is a joke, but no. We have actually had to turn arguments about what free speech is, into something we can resolve in pleasant ways. I have to say it improved neither the sex nor my understanding of free speech. I do, however, think we all have to talk about it, even if we don't know what it means. My heavily revised piece follows. The reader may feel that there is a contradiction between its exhortations and the story of how it has taken its present form. I hope the words still carry the same weight as they did, even though the history of their coming to be on this page may seem to belie that.

In the early nineties I wrote a book — this book — which examined various high profile cheating scandals in bridge. In a nutshell, I suggested that maybe the people accused of cheating hadn't been, that the chiefly American accusers might be wrong as a consequence of strong cultural differences between their understanding of bridge and those of other nationalities. I also suggested that Ely Culbertson might have deliberately destroyed a competitor for the big money at stake in the 1930s by creating the idea that he was cheating. I sent this book to several publishers and was prepared for polite declinations. I was not expecting what actually happened, which was that I received vitriolic angry rejections. My book was being censored by mainstream publishers; their problem wasn't whether it would sell, but they hated the ideas in it. What could I do? I thought I'd produced a good book that would sell, but I put it in a drawer and moved on. One day, however, I mentioned it to a top Australian player who asked if he could look at it. He took it home and brought it back first thing in the morning. Damn, I thought. It wasn't any good after all, if he hasn't even bothered reading it. But in fact what had happened was that he sat up all night with it, and we now spent some hours talking about how wonderful he thought it was. He thought I should keep trying to get it published. I sent it to the editor of a UK magazine who serialised it. Then I self-published it.

Although it received nice reviews, soon after its release, the influential magazine *Bridge World* published a hostile editorial about it. A reader sent in a meek attempt to defend the book and that attracted more editorial anger. Wow, two hostile editorials. I could rest assured that I really had written something worthwhile at that point. Nobody else wrote to *Bridge World* to support me after that. Meanwhile, the edition quickly sold out and I started getting feedback from people which was unexpected and completely the opposite from the tone of criticism that appeared in *Bridge World*. More than one person said it had been life-changing for them and they really meant it. It let them be more tolerant to others, to be less paranoid and angry about other people. Many people read it in a night. Somebody wrote to say he'd stayed up all night reading it and went down to a shop to buy three more copies to give people the next day. A bridge partnership stayed up all night reading it aloud to each other. Non-bridge players read it. I was invited to present a talk to a magicians' convention in Vegas. Ten years or more later I still occasionally received these mails.

Lots of people wrote to say that they agreed with what I'd said.

But not one person wrote in public that they agreed with it.

Who could blame them when they saw what had happened to the first poor devil who made a stab at it in *Bridge World*?

Some years later came another development. One of the ex-world champion US players, who was a prominent accuser of others being cheats, published an autobiography in which he presented various evidence to support his case. Trouble is, some of his evidence was factually incorrect. Whether by mistake or not, he had materially changed the stories of played hands in ways that made it look worse for those accused. I collected together both his stories and, from official records, what actually happened in each case, wrote it up and sent it to *Bridge World*. It may not surprise you to hear that it declined to publish my article, but it surprised me. Now, this was surely an intrinsically interesting story — 'world champ lies in book, were the Italians REALLY cheating?' — and yet he claimed that people weren't interested. Please consider this. If all those people who wrote privately to me to support me had done it in public, the editor would most certainly not have been able to use this as his excuse. Meanwhile it has gone into history, this false evidence used to accuse some truly great players of cheating. Silence has consequences.

This was brought back to my mind recently, reading of a small business called booklocker.com.

The proprietor filed a class action lawsuit against Amazon on the grounds that Amazon was attempting to force POD publishers to agree that they had to pay Amazon to print their books. Her brave story is available online.[45] She fought on her own. It could have been a victory for many. Instead nobody else joined her. They were

---

[45]http://antitrust.booklocker.com

too scared to speak up. "We were basically thrown to the wolves, and had to publicly fight on our own, with many publishers whispering to us in the background, but not publicly joining us on the front lines."

Silence has consequences. It is not neutral. And speaking where nobody can hear you — or where the people who need to hear you won't — that might as well be silence.

So this review is addressed more than anything to people who may be in doubt about what is going on here at Goodreads, but are scared to speak, nervous to speak, or perhaps simply don't understand why it might be important.

SPEAK!!! Don't be bullied. Not by GR management. Not by the protesters. Say what you think. If you disagree with GR management they will be unfailingly polite, whereas the free speech advocates can say what they like, how they like, where they like. And some of them do! Okay. Still speak! They are maybe a bit sharper with a pen than you are? So what. Still speak. I have no idea if speaking up is ever a right, but it is surely sometimes a duty and I really think this is a case where it is a duty. How you are treated when you do, doesn't really matter. Those who disagree with you might tell you to fuck off, call you toxic — that's their definition of free speech. But live by yours. In the end that is all free speech can be: what YOU think it is. Not what GR managment thinks. Not what Manny thinks. What YOU think. That is, it is what we each think, which makes it, of course, a right dog's breakfast.

But if you are doing this, exercising your right to free speech in a closed room on your own with the lights off, either through fear, or because other people have told you that you can say what you like but NOT where it counts, I assure you that this is not free speech, even if the free speechers tell you so. If that was free speech, well, Soviet Russia was its most loyal supporter. There, after all, you weren't stopped from saying what you thought, only from saying it where anybody was listening. There is no difference between a bureaucracy telling you where you can say something and a bunch of people on GR telling you that. The effect is the same.

I am reminded of what happened recently in the much publicised situation of Colin McGinn. A group of academics stated in a public letter[46] that "We recognize Dr. McGinn's right to free speech" but then went on to describe the ways in which it should be circumscribed. He was at perfect liberty to talk about anything that didn't actually matter to him. At the moment, you have more rights to free speech than this, and a great duty to use them. This ad appears on Amazon as I write:

> **Forum Moderator**
>
> We like to think of our forums as a Free-Speech Zone. And freedom works best at the point of a bayonet — or a "Delete Post" button. As Forum Moderator, it'll be your job to keep the forums safe and sanitary, while highlighting the posts that actually have something valuable to say. You'll slap the bad guys' hands and the good guys' backs.[47]

If you are tired of Hydra, if you are thinking it doesn't really matter if such and such is deleted, keep in mind that this is really what you are fighting about. 'Safe and sanitary' scares the bejesus out of me. I can't distinguish it from something you'd see in a Soviet Russia or Communist China re-education camp. But that's just my opinion. PLEASE HAVE YOURS. And please remember that it doesn't really count if nobody can hear it.

---

[46] http://feministphilosophers.wordpress.com/2013/07/18/letter-from-concerned-philosophers/

[47] http://www.amazon.com/gp/jobs/230906/ref=j_sr_16_t?ie=UTF8&category=*&jobSearchKeywords=speeches&location=*&page=1

A Review of "The Wonderful O"

This book was one of my favorites when I was about eight, and I read it over and over again, as eight-year-olds do. I can still remember many passages verbatim. In case you don't know it, here is a brief summary of the plot. Two disreputable pirates, Black and Littlejack, arrive on the island of Ooroo. They have reason to believe that a fabulous treasure is buried there. They also have an insane hatred of the letter O.

They proceed to search for the treasure, and also to ban everything that contains an O in its name: clocks, dogs, boxes, whatever. The terrified inhabitants of the island are forced to speak an O-less language. They plan a revolt (or possibly a rebellion or a revolution). One of the theoretical questions which occupies their spare time is that of determining what the most important of the banned O-words is. Is it 'love' or 'honour' or 'valour'?

In the end, they win their fight, and they realize that, great as all these words are, none of them was the greatest.

The greatest O-word is FREEDOM.

Afterword

One of the hardest parts of collecting this book has been figuring out how to write this afterword. I've been alternately staring at a cursor and writing paragraphs of what I feel are tangents and digressions, unable to formulate a coda. The contributors are all clear in at least one goal of this book, which is this: to create an indelible document of our experiences and opinions regarding the policy change at Goodreads and the review deletions that followed. It's a taxidermy of a conflict, sewing up the wounds and straightening the bowtie on the cadaver of a corner of the Goodreads community. Each individual record is by nature individual, and we don't even agree with each other in places. This document does not aim to speak for all, and only maps the smallest part of a specific time in the changing community that makes up Goodreads.

It has been noted many times that this is a tempest in a teapot, but this is our corner of our teapot, and here is where we have scried the leaves. We have undertaken compiling this collection partially because of the fundamental ephemerality of the Internet. Sometimes ephemerality is a good thing, as least where it pertains to the documentation of the off-handed and the ill-considered things we all sometimes say, and especially online. I have been reviewing on Goodreads for five years now, and there are certain reviews that I wince at when I see them again. I don't even agree with myself anymore, my opinions and perspective having changed in the years since I wrote down my thoughts on a book. Goodreads is both a real time conversation, and an archive of those conversations, and the archive is often incomplete because of the nature of the Internet record.

But when the review deletions started, that very ephemerality took an ominous turn, not just the inevitable bubbling of conversation that people pop into and out of, but this chilling intrusion for reasons that were not clear, and have not been made clear to the satisfaction of many. What many of us wanted when most of these pieces were written was a clear dialogue with Goodreads. Not many of us believe anymore we will get one, and the protests have one by one fallen silent as people left the site, decided to stop reviewing on Goodreads, or just decided the policy wasn't so onerous they couldn't live within it. Goodreads has been, for many of us, a beloved community, one that has been materially damaged by this conflict.

The other thing I can say about this collection is that no one intends this to be a revenge piece, sharpening the knives of our discontent at the expense of Goodreads. So much of the anger expressed in this collection comes from a place of real love for the Goodreads community, and the hurt that came out of so much of this conflict. Beyond the fighting on the feedback thread or the nose-thumbing protests, there were sometimes heated quarrels between users about tactics, methods, ideology, the concept of reviewing itself, or even old grudges. Many of these arguments were, in the parlance of our times, off-topic, but still important exercises in community. We were a community in crisis, and in many ways, we still are.

Some of us have given up and gone elsewhere. Some of us are tired of the discussion, and are waiting to see if Goodreads can sort this out their own. Some of us have hope that Goodreads is listening, and that a dialogue is possible. Which one I am varies minute by minute. This is a recording of a moment in time, and that is the only thing we can agree on. This lack of collective coda is in some ways a fitting tribute to the community I loved, because argument and the cacophony of voices was what I found so thrilling about Goodreads. As the voices fall silent, the individuals who make up the amorphous and always changing community must decide for themselves, as they always have. I can't write a coda because I can't speak for others. I can only and ever speak for myself.

Ceridwen Christensen
Minneapolis, November 1, 2013

Index

1001 Books You Must Read Before You Die, 147
120 journées de Sodome, Les, 141

253, 48

Adams, Abigail, 164
Adams, John, 161
AdBlocker, 127
algorithms, 129
Amazon, viii, 4, 11, 75, 82, 84, 93, 95, 102, 127, 139, 170, 180, 182
Amish, 116
Archimedes, 103
assholes, 17, 34, 82, 130
Austen, Jane, 4
author behavior, ix, 17, 71, 121

Banks, Russell, 52
Banned Books Week, 130
Bared to You, 4
Bath, K.P., 74
bears, 141
Bertens, H., 34
Bezos, Jeff, 4, 102
Big Bang, 16
Big Six, 28
Black Death, 16
Black Ice, 22
Blonde, 53

bondage, 93
book-burning, 44
BookLikes, 7, 118, 126, 143, 155
booklocker.com, 180
Bradbury, Ray, 136
Bransford, Nathan, 9
bridge, 178
Bridge World, 179
Brown, Patrick, 6, 75
Bryson, Bill, 4
Bulgakov, Mikhail, 60
Burr, 52
Burr, Aaron, 161

California, 73, 165
Card, Orson Scott, 23, 35, 49, 73
Carla, 26
Carter, Asa Earl, 73
censorship, 16, 34, 45, 54, 56, 57, 83, 118, 130
Ceridwen, 151
Chandler, Otis, 9, 22, 82, 127
Chicken Chicken, 148
child pornography, 23
Christ, Jesus, 16, 134
Christy, 144, 145
Civil Disobedience and Other Essays, 132
Clouds, 109
CNN, 77
compromise, 84

Concord, 11
Continental Drift, 52
Cornell, 171
crap, 48
creationism, 133
Crystal Vision, 53
Culbertson, Ely, 179
cyberbullying, 84

data mining, 12
deconstruction, 103
Denver, 11
Derrida, Jacques, 104
Destruction of Dresden, The, 43
dickheads, 177
dicks, 40
dogs, 51
Douglas, William O., 162
downvoting, 23
doxing, 23
Dresden, 43
Drive, 68
dummies, 118

Editorial, 56
Elizabeth, 151
Emmanuelle, 93
Erickson, Kara, ix, 6, 17, 78, 130
Eureka, 94, 103
Evnine, Simon, 54
Evslin, Bernard, 104

*F*CK*, 16
Facebook, 119
Fair Play or Foul?, 177
fake names, 119
Feedback group, 17, 22, 32, 127
fellatio, 148
feminism, 35
Fifty Shades of Grey, 24, 93, 141

Fire Upon the Deep, A, 53
First Amendment, 11, 162
Fitzpatrick's, Becca, 22
flagging, 91
Forbes, 171
Forbes 25 Top Reviewers, 127
foreplay, 178
Founding Fathers, 160
Franklin, Benjamin, 160
free speech, 11, 161, 178
French, 141, 145
fuck, 16

G+, 119
Game of Thrones, A, 144
Gass, William H., 53
Gazelle, 116
Gibson's Bookstore, 11
GIFs, 101
Gleichschaltung, 117
Godzilla, 107
Goldilocks, 141
Goldman, Ron, 45
Google, 119
Goosebumps, 147
Gospel according to Saint Mark, The, 4
gottlieb, brian, 138
Graham, Arthur, x, 56, 108
Great Goodreads Censorship Debacle, The, 108
Grisham, John, 177

Hamilton, Alexander, 161
hate speech, 163
Heaven, 160
Hell, 161
Hemings, Sally, 164
Henry, Patrick, 160
Hercules, 94

hidden reviews, 19
Hitler, Adolf, 36, 40–42, 72
Holland, 148
Holmes, Oliver Wendell, 162
Holocaust denial, 42
homophobia, 23
Houellebecq, Michel, 51
How We Decide, 74
Howard, Lauren Pippa, 9, 76
Hydra, x, 94, 99, 101, 104, 106, 132, 151, 160, 173, 182
hyperlink, 104

incest, 141
Inquisition, Spanish, 58
iPads, 103, 141
Irving, David, 42, 49, 73

Jackson, Percy, 4
James, E.L., 141
Jaruzelski, Wojciech, 57
Jefferson, Thomas, 160
JennyJen, 26
Josey Wales: Two Westerns, 73

Kemper, 73
Kennedy, John F., 110
Kindle, 4, 68
Kowalski, David, 138
Krantz, Judith, 141
Ku Klux Klan, 73

Lahiri, Jhumpa, 52
Lehrer, Jonah, 74
lesbianism, 141
libel, 163
librarians, 8, 143
LibraryThing, 134, 143
Lipstadt, Deborah, 43
literary criticism, 34

lizard overlords, 84
logic, 54, 55, 109
Logic: A Very Short Introduction, 50
Lord of the Flies, 139, 149
Lowland, The, 52

Madison, James, 160
Man and Superman, 135
Mao Tsetong, 41
Mark, 92
markets, 161
martial law, 57
Martian Way, The, 93
Martin, G.R.R, 145
Marxism, 35
Massachusetts, 175
Massachusetts Literary Journal, 61
Master and Margarita, The, 60
masturbation, 51
Matthew, Saint, 134
McGinn, Colin, 182
McGoodreader, G.R., x, 108
Mein Kampf, ix, 36, 40, 42, 72, 92, 135
Meskis, Joyce, 11
Mike, 40, 42, 72
Miranda, 24, 26
Mishima, Yukio, 109
mommyporn, 141
Monroe, Marilyn, 53
Moskowitz, Hannah, 8
Mosquito Coast, The, 52
Moving for Dummies, 118
MySpace, 119

Narnia, 148
New York Times, 171
Niemöller, Martin, 83
Ninth Circuit Court of Appeals, 165

nudity, 56, 82
Nutting, Alissa, 51

Oates, Joyce Carol, 53
Obama, Michelle, 56
Odyssey, The, 4
off-topic, ix, 50, 62, 121, 132, 141, 144, 145, 149
Ohio, 163
Oklahoma, 163
Omensetter's Luck, 53
Orwell, George, 50

Paine, Thomas, 163
panty-sniffing, 56
Patriot Act, 11
Paul, 91
pedophilia, 74
philosophy, 54
plagiarism, 23, 74
Platform, 51
Poland, 57
Portrait of a Lady, The, 144
postmodernism, 48, 103
Pride and Prejudice, 4
Princess Daisy, 141
Principia Mathematica, 109
print on demand, 180
printing, 160
Proposition 8, 73
Proust Was a Neuroscientist, 74
pulled-to-publish, 24
Putting Linguistics into Speech Recognition, 54

queer theory, 35
Quicksilver, 93
Quotations from Chairman Mao Tse-tung, 41

racism, 23

rameau, 24
rape, 76, 84, 109, 133, 141
rationality, 54
Rayner, Manny, 54, 73
resistors, 58
rhubarb, 110
Roth, Veronica, 7
Rousseau, Jean-Jacques, 168
Rowson, Martin, 16
Russell, Bertrand, 93, 109

Sade, Marquis de, 141
sales, 68
Sales, Leila, 149
Salon, 9
Sandusky, Jerry, 74
Secret of Castle Cant, The, 74
September Girls, 9
sex
    anal, 76, 93, 109
    and free speech, 178
    in books, 133
    in Jane Austen, 4
    on cover, 51
    oral, 148
shelves, 7, 17, 34, 75
shit
    and giggles, 10
    hitting fan, 7
    horse, 82
    miserable, 83
Short History of Everything, A, 4
Simpson, Nicole, 45
Simpson, O.J., 45
Sinclair, Steph, 74
slander, 161
slash fiction, 6
Social Contract, The, 168
Solidarity, 59
Sorrentino, Gilbert, 53

Sparks, Nicholas, 144
STGRB, 30, 56, 84
Stine, R.L., 148

Tampa, 50
Tattered Cover, 11
Terms of Use, 36, 45, 56, 57, 75, 84,
    90, 120, 133, 143, 151, 164
Theroux, Paul, 52
This Song Will Save Your Life, 149
Thurber, James, 183
Tolstoy, Lev, 152
Twilight, 4, 93
Twitter, 119

Uncommon Whore, An, 92
unconscionability, 166

vampires, 4
Varma, Nandakishore, 111
Vidal, Gore, 52
Vinge, Vernor, 53
Virginia, 175

Wallace, George, 73
Washington Post, ix, 9, 40, 95
Washington, George, 161
werewolves, 4
Whack-a-Mole, 100
Whitehead, Alfred North, 109
Wikipedia, 42, 130
Wind-Up Bird Chronicle, The, 91
Wonderful O, The, 183

YA, 101, 138
YA Highway, 7
Yale, 171
Yes, I Farted, 108

zombies, 51

www.ingramcontent.com/pod-product-compliance
Lightning Source LLC
LaVergne TN
LVHW041631060526
838200LV00040B/1533